Lost Restaurants

OF

CHICAGO

Lost Restaurants
OF
CHICAGO

GREG BORZO

AMERICAN PALATE

Published by American Palate
A Division of The History Press
Charleston, SC
www.historypress.com

Front cover, top middle: Doug Sohn.

First published 2018

Manufactured in the United States

ISBN 9781625859334

Library of Congress Control Number: 2018952865

To my nieces and nephews: Paula, Theresa, Cecilia, Peter Chris, Nicole, Colin, Peter
Benjamin, Sarah, Oliver and Alex. You guys are great! May you stand together forever.

Contents

Foreword

When reminiscing about their city and the restaurants they miss, Chicagoans will talk forlornly about such revered icons as The Bakery, Jacques, Don Roth's Blackhawk (I still often quote the tagline "tossed three times so as not to bruise the tender leaves" whenever I'm making a salad), Le Perroquet and other beacons of fine dining.

Not me. When I'm asked about which restaurant I miss, I only have one answer: the stand-up hot dog counter at the Woolworth's on the Magnificent Mile.

Located on the 600 block of North Michigan Avenue, the five-and-dime store Woolworth's was my Target. It's where I bought my school supplies and Tootsie Rolls, where I looked confusingly at the canaries and turtles for sale in the back of the store, where I bought my Cubs hat in 1977 (and wore it until I retired it in 2016 because, well, you know why) and, most importantly, where I stood at the counter in the window facing the street eating hot dogs (mustard only, please) and a bag of Jay's potato chips and drank an icy Coca-Cola through a striped paper straw. Nirvana.

I stood next to bus drivers and cops, moms with toddlers—which was once my mom and me—professionals in suits and ties, shoppers and pretty much anyone who lived in Chicago back then. It was quick, easy and delicious. Woolworth's had a sit-down restaurant with stools, a wavy counter and a server who brought your food to you. But that was too fancy. I preferred the stand-up place with the hot dogs heating as they rolled back and forth on the metal contraption that was designed solely to cook wieners.

Doug Sohn, founder of Hot Doug's, Chicago's Sausage Superstore, made an art of crafting, selling and celebrating encased meats. *Doug Sohn.*

We all miss our favorite restaurants. We miss the familiarity. We miss knowing exactly how our favorite dish is going to taste. We miss seeing the same staff each time we go in. We would look at the menu knowing full well what was on it and knowing full well what we were going to order. We miss seeing ourselves when we were younger.

Before my family moved downtown when I was around twelve years old, we lived in Deerfield. Back in the '60s, that was pretty much like living in the country. And the food scene may have been worse. There were the Italian restaurants in Highwood, like My Favorite Inn, that we'd go to a few times each year and where I'd order plain spaghetti with butter. But for the most part, the suburbs truly constituted a food desert.

Back then, the dining highlight for me was every Sunday night when we would get dinner from Don the Cantonese Chef. It was take-out only with a small opening where they would hand you your order in a brown grocery bag, and there were a couple of plastic chairs where you could sit and wait. It also had this totally cool—at least that's what I thought—Coke machine where the glass bottles laid on their sides. You put your coin in the slot (I'm guessing it was a dime), opened the glass door and pulled the bottle straight out. You had to drink it there and place your empty

Hot Doug's fans were so enthralled with the restaurant that many of them had the restaurant's logo tattooed on their arms, legs…and unmentionable places. *Doug Sohn.*

bottle in the crate next to the machine. The egg foo yung was pretty good too, as I recall. Most importantly, I'd take the little bag of crunchy chow mein noodles with me to snack on while watching L.A. T-Birds roller derby and Bob Luce professional wrestling on TV.

And then we moved to the big city. Chicago back then was most definitely not the dining destination it is today. Back then, fine dining often meant you would get pineapple slices on your steak, and a wedge salad was called a salad. Or there were fancy French restaurants like the aforementioned Jacques and Le Perroquet. We never went to those; they must have been thought of as too exotic. We did go to Kon Tiki Ports, and there was a Mandarin restaurant whose name I can't remember. I guess that was about as "exotic" as we could handle.

I'm happy to say that those days are long over. I can now brag that I live in one of the great restaurant cities in the world. And yet, there are lots of restaurants that are no longer with us and that I miss dearly: Charmets; the Belden Deli; Lance's; Burt's (which is now the Wiener's Circle but was a lot less crowded and a lot more peaceful back then); Moto, where I first experienced how funny and clever food could be; the Drake Hotel drugstore; and the amazing Star Top Café on North Lincoln Avenue that was the first restaurant to genuinely challenge me and open up the possibilities of what a restaurant could be.

Oh yeah, I kinda miss Hot Doug's, too. There's a rumor going around that it's mentioned somewhere later on in this book. I'm genuinely flattered to be a part of such wonderful company.

I could really go for a Woolworth's hot dog right about now.

—Doug Sohn
Founder of Hot Doug's, the Sausage Superstore and
Encased Meat Emporium (2001–14)

Acknowledgements

Chicago has so many bygone restaurants that starting this project was intimidating. Which ones to include? Who to interview? What to read?

A wealth of people helped me pull this book together, and I'm deeply grateful to all of them for their assistance. Many restaurateurs, historians, food critics, authors, bloggers and other experts shared stories, knowledge and experiences. Chief among them was Eric Bronsky, an author, Chicago restaurant historian and collector of restaurant paraphernalia. Eric provided invaluable insights, innumerable suggestions, impressive editing skills and photographs, all of which greatly enhanced this book. Long may you continue to enjoy your passion for Chicago restaurants, in terms of their histories as well as their food.

A few restaurateurs really stood out. Early in the project, Gordon Sinclair was quick to respond to my questions and generous with his time. Later on, Marc Schulman was especially enthusiastic about the book and willing to provide everything that was asked of him. Jeff Thomas was helpful. But most of all, Doug Sohn was extremely responsive and supportive. He was so interesting and easy to speak with that I asked him to write the foreword to this book. I was glad he said "yes," impressed when he beat the deadline and delighted with his contribution.

It was exciting and extremely rewarding to talk with and work with these and other restaurateurs. They gave me a good sense of what their work is all about. It was an honor to have met them.

A special thanks to Ben Gibson, commissioning editor at The History Press, for proposing that I write this book. I appreciate Ben's confidence in me. Like he promised, the book has been a great opportunity and surprisingly fun to work on. Throughout the process, I certainly learned a lot about food, restaurants and Chicago.

Senior editor Hilary Parrish was great to work with. And although I can't name the rest of the team at The History Press, they are all easy to work with as well as efficient, productive and talented at what they do.

Part of writing any book about restaurants happily involves eating out a lot. This was true even for a book about *lost* restaurants because many existing restaurants can inform a writer or historian about what was out there before and which lost restaurants to include. My wife, Christine Bertrand, was always willing to accompany me in this "research." Her good taste and knowledge of food helped me sort out what to look for and what contemporary restaurants can teach us about their bygone brother and sister restaurants. Her overall support throughout the process kept me going.

Library research was a little less enjoyable than restaurant "research," but it was even more rewarding, especially with the help of several of Chicago's top-notch librarians: Lesley Martin at the Chicago History Museum's Research Center; Julie Lynch at the Chicago Public Library's Sulzer Regional Library; and Morag Walsh at the Harold Washington Library Center's Special Collections and Preservation Division. These three angels have helped me on many of my previous books, and their knowledge and professionalism never cease to amaze me.

This may sound odd, but I would like to acknowledge the technology that increasingly facilitates the work of authors. The tools we now have available are extremely powerful, even compared to just a few years ago. Here I'm talking about searchable online newspaper archives (sure beats the old days of microfilm); online maps that act as directories (sure beats the old Yellow Pages); affordable-high resolution cameras; faster, more powerful Internet connectivity; hard-to-find books that are now easy to find and read (through Google Books and other online sources); mega databases and

The "Auf Wiedersehen" sign outside Zum Deutschen Eck in 2000 speaks for the thousands of Chicago's great bygone restaurants. *Robert W. Krueger photo. Chicago Public Library, Northside Neighborhood History Collection.*

image repositories, such as the Chicago Connection and John Chuckman's Collection; online postcard collections, such as the Curt Teich Postcard Archives Collection at the Newberry Library; and commercial sites, such as Card Cow, that helped me visualize old restaurants that I had never visited. It's a wonderful time to be writing about history.

Many restaurant lovers and Chicago history fans helped by providing photos of and/or stories about their favorite restaurants. This includes Judy Anneaux (Rotunno Family Collection), Stephanie Barto (administrative coordinator at the Rogers Park/West Ridge Historical Society), Rich Beddome, Christine Bertrand, David Borzo, Paul Borzo, Sherry Brenner, Wendy Bright (WendyCityChicago blog and tours), Beth Montcalm Campe, Emily Clark (Lettuce Entertain You Enterprises), Fe Fernandez, Mimi Ferrara (Rotunno Family Collection), Louise Gregg, Debby and Philip Halpern, John Holden, Janet Hong, Christopher Lynch, Mary May (Department of Cultural Affairs and Special Events), Doug and Jane Swanson Nystrom, Margaret O'Connell, John Brook O'Neal, Wes Pope, Herb Russel, Cyndi Schacher, Patrick Steffes, Shannon Tauschman (Lawry's The Prime Rib), Monique Tranchevent and Jan Whitaker (Restaurant-ing Through History blog). There were many others who assisted, but space limitations do not allow me to mention all of them here. But I will single out Art Peterson, who had already helped with images for two of my previous books and came through again, even at the last minute. Such generosity and collegiality!

Librarians at the following organizations did a Herculean job of tracking down, scanning and sending me restaurant images, of which the book holds about 120: Ryerson and Burnham Libraries at the Art Institute of Chicago; Research Center at the Chicago History Museum; Crerar Library at the University of Chicago; Richard J. Daley Library at the University of Illinois at Chicago; Special Collections and Preservation Division at the Harold Washington Library Center; Rogers Park/West Ridge Historical Society; Chicago Public Library's Sulzer Regional Library; and Curt Teich Postcard Archives Collection at the Newberry Library.

To all of you I say, "Merci buckets!"

"No Longer Taking Reservations"

When it comes to restaurants, Chicago is the City of Big Choices. It's the ultimate foodie town. What other city can boast that it's named after a food, in this case the small wild onions that grew in profusion along the region's riverbanks?

Over the years, Chicago's dynamic and varied restaurants have defined the city, fed and entertained millions, drawn people together and helped the city grow and develop. Most of them, however, have been "86ed," a restaurant term for a menu item that has been discontinued. And yet while these establishments—whether holes-in-the-walls or starched-white-tablecloth dining rooms—may be gone, they're not forgotten. They won our hearts and minds—and stomachs. They served up plate after plate, block after block of good food and priceless memories. They embody a vast smorgasbord of fascinating people and places, history and hysterics, décors, designs and dishes.

Running a restaurant is tough work. Experts estimate that half of all restaurants close within their first year. That means tens of thousands of superb, trendsetting, inviting, fun or just plain crazy restaurants have come and gone since Chicago was founded in 1833.

Why did some stay open a century or more, while others faltered within a few months? Prohibition did some in. Others were closed by the health department. Still others simply ran their course or fell behind changing tastes. Like athletes, some quit at the top of their game, while others lingered on life support for years before putting up the closed-for-good sign.

Won Kow in Chinatown was Chicago's oldest continuously operating Chinese restaurant until it closed in 2018. *Eric Bronsky.*

A quick look at some "dearly departed" restaurants that died as this book was being born identifies some surprising reasons why restaurants close. One of the most unusual reasons is the story behind the shuttering of Monastero's Ristorante & Banquets (3935 West Devon Avenue). Opened in 1967, this successful place went out on a high note in 2017 when an offer—apparently too good to refuse—for its property came out of the blue (or perhaps from above). Monastero's sold its property to the Elim Romanian Pentecostal Church so the group could build a new church and community center. Why that spot? Church leaders wanted the property because a study had concluded that Monastero's was at the geographic center of their congregation.

A restaurant that closed to a "standing ovation"—literally, with an eight-hour-long line out the door—was Hot Doug's (3324 North California Avenue). This tremendously popular sausage superstore closed in 2014 after just thirteen years. But don't say "just" to owner Doug Sohn, who worked there virtually every day the restaurant was open and personally greeted almost every customer. "I had the opportunity to close because I could, not because I had to, and that's rare in the restaurant business," Sohn said.

Schaller's Original Pump (3714 South Halsted Street) also closed recently but had a much longer history than Hot Doug's. ("Pump" in its name referred to the beer that was pumped in from a brewery next door.) Thought to be Chicago's longest continuously running tavern, this once proud place closed in 2017 after 136 years. That's old enough to have sported liquor license number six, served visitors to the World's Columbian Exposition of 1893 and hosted celebrations for all three Chicago White Sox World Series wins.

This horse cart was an attractive fixture at Monastero's, which closed on short notice due to an unexpected offer to buy the property. *Eric Bronsky.*

Located across the street from the legendary Eleventh Ward Democratic Party headquarters in Bridgeport, Schaller's catered to politicos, particularly the Daley clan. It was also popular with laborers, cops and city workers. "If you wanted to see anyone from the neighborhood, you'd come here," Elmer Mestrovic told the *Tribune* the day Schaller's closed. The sixty-year-old neighborhood resident had been going to the tavern since he was a toddler, but there weren't enough locals like him who were loyal to Schaller's fading eating and drinking culture. Another reason the tavern closed is that it was hit with high property taxes after ninety-two-year-old Jack Schaller, who lived upstairs, died in 2016. This caused the tavern to lose tax exemptions that had been "grandfathered in" to the owner.

In 2017, the South Loop also lost its oldest and most famous restaurant, Blackie's (Polk and Clark Streets). It was a playground for movie stars and celebrities, from Lena Horne to the Rat Pack. The Marx Brothers and Three Stooges stopped in frequently, once reportedly getting into a food fight. "Alas, no one in the family wanted to continue running it," said Jeff Thomas, the fourth-generation owner from 1976 to the closing. "The restaurant business requires an enormous amount of time and work."

One of the happiest restaurant endings came in 2005 when Eli Schulman closed his restaurant to refocus on cheesecake, his most popular dessert. *Marc Schulman.*

Won Kow (2237 South Wentworth Avenue) was another family-run restaurant that recently closed up shop, in part because no one in the family was interested in the long hours required to run it. Opened in 1928, this Chinatown mainstay was Chicago's oldest continuously operating Chinese restaurant. After ninety years, it was easy to take Won Kow for granted, but the building's stone guardian lions (also known as fu dogs) were not enough to protect the business. Chicago will miss its chop suey, chow mein and egg foo yung but also the more authentic Chinese dishes, including bird's nest soup, orange chicken and dim sum.

Another ethnic community lost its favorite restaurant, Chicago Brauhaus, at the end of 2017, this time after fifty-two years of suds and sauerbraten. It was a true Deutsch treat. Brothers Harry

A Bridgeport hangout for pols and police, Schaller's survived for 136 years. In 2016, the year before it closed, the 92-year-old owner, Jack Schaller, lived upstairs. *Eric Bronsky.*

and Guenter Kempf maintained this old-world holdout in the heart of Lincoln Square, once part of a thriving German American community. The restaurant served large portions of hearty, traditional German food to the sound of oom-pah-pah bands. Sometimes the musicians would even lead customers dancing outside into the Lincoln Square mall. The brothers may have tired of running a restaurant for so long, but their name will live on, as the city renamed the square in front of the now shuttered restaurant "Kempf Plaza."

A whole book could be written about the names of lost restaurants. Some were literal (Not Just Pasta), while others were funny or even goofy. Here are some favorites: Gable on Clark, Doctor Jazz and Great Gritzbe's Flying Food Show (renamed Not-So-Great Gritzbe's after it didn't do so great). There was Mondays…and Fridays. Club Lucky… and Hemingway's Movable Feast. Flaming Sally's…and Dingbats. The Pump Room was named after the Pump Room Restaurant in Bath, one of the English city's most stylish spots. Gordon Sinclair said he left the *'s* off the name of his restaurant, Gordon, to shave twenty-five dollars off the sign painter's bill.

A 1931 menu cover from Henrici's, Chicago's most revered fine dining restaurant, expresses style and grace. *Chicago History Museum.*

Meanwhile, menus of bygone restaurants also deserve their own tome. Although usually not given more than a glance, menus speak volumes about their restaurants, displaying class, mediocrity or poor taste. The menu covers for Henrici's and Nanking expressed elegance and sophistication, while Hyde Park's House of Tiki's menu had layer after layer of stickers, reflecting price increases.

Menus reveal the prices of yesteryear. In 1944, a triple-decker sandwich cost $0.30 at B/G Foods, but in 1979, braised steak strips of African lion (with Grand Marnier sauce) cost $16.00 at Café Bohemia.

Also, menus set out the rules. "Extra charge for all Meals or Desserts taken to Rooms," said the 1856 menu at the Foster House, a boardinghouse. Or, "No ladies welcome," read the menu in a number of Chicago's nineteenth-century restaurants.

Chicago is especially privileged to have so many ethnic restaurants. Many of them were opened by immigrants who arrived with empty stomachs but worked miracles to fill the stomach of hungry Americans, not only hungry for food but also interested in learning about other peoples, experiencing their traditions and tasting their cooking. If we are what we eat, then Chicagoans are a wonderful spicy mélange of cultures.

Restaurants feed body and soul, and the ones we've lost can give us a taste

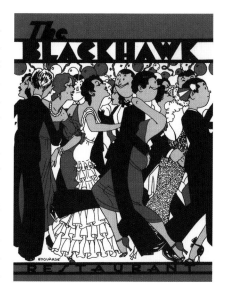

The Blackhawk, next to the Loop "L," could be Chicago's most favorite bygone restaurant. This menu cover indicates class and sophistication. *University of Illinois at Chicago Library.*

of where we've been and who we are. Let's take a trip down memory lane to see which bygone restaurants you remember and which ones you might have missed out on. Your table's waiting...

CHAPTER 1

Extraordinary Eateries

F or loads of fun, diners in the 1980s and '90s would "air their dirty laundry" at the SaGa Laundry Bar & Café at Southport and Newport Avenues. Not only could they eat and drink at the laundromat, but they could also watch a light board to tell them when their wash or dry cycle had finished. Thus, customers could handle their laundry during lunch or dinner, thereby avoiding the boredom often associated with watching one's laundry tumble or spin around.

SaGa was also a modest museum of laundry paraphernalia and memorabilia: antique washing machines, irons, posters and soapboxes. The combination of food and laundry—as well as the abandoned bras, panties, shorts and unpaired socks pinned to a corkboard—must have sparked many conversations, and maybe even some romances.

This is just one of a stupendous smorgasbord of extraordinary eateries that Chicagoans have seen come and go. Some sported a wild and crazy décor while others served exquisite food in an elegant setting. Others expressed ethnic pride or culinary trends. Chicagoans can fondly recall bygone restaurants for striking views and silly gimmicks; thick, juicy steaks and vegetarian delights; hooch during Prohibition and exotic cocktails afterward; and gourmet encased meat but also franks served by felons. Consider this chapter your appetizers for a multi-course progressive dinner at the Windy City's most significant, delicious or downright outlandish restaurants.

Let's get into the swing of things with Flo's Restaurant and Cocktail Parlour, which featured a trapeze artist performing in front of a building

Math Igler's Casino, with its famed singing waiters decked out in lederhosen, anchored Lakeview's German American community. *Eric Bronsky.*

at 17 West Randolph Street. An attractive young woman would swing back and forth in a lit-up, cutout section of the building that ran about four stories high. She would wear spiked heels and "a one-piece outfit like the bunnies did at the old Playboy clubs," according to Joey Airdo, who had a friend who held onto this job for a while.

Flo's come-on may have been designed to make up for the fact that the food was "unremarkable," according to author and restaurant historian Eric Bronsky, who ate there during the '60s and '70s. At least it served good fruit pie, particularly the strawberry and gooseberry, although that was a bit odd for a place with a racy spectacle out front. In fact, the big sign in front of the restaurant advertised "Lucy's Pies" right under the words "Cocktail Parlour." The restaurant closed after the building was destroyed by fire in 1980 and demolished soon thereafter, along with the rest of Block 37.

"Big Jim" Colosimo, who founded Chicago's Outfit, took great pride in his restaurant, located in the Levy, but rival gangsters killed him there. *Author's collection.*

Diners enjoyed a different version of this stunt at Texas de Brazil (51 East Ohio Street), which opened in 2008. Female aerial wine stewards would swing on a trapeze through the restaurant's forty-foot-high vertical wine cellar to fetch bottles of wine for customers. These incredibly graceful Cirque du Soleil–like acrobats could twist and twirl, flip and fly—whatever it took to retrieve a bottle from among the 1,400 choices of wine without disturbing its content. "Order one from the top," suggested a guest of the author, hoping for a bit of a show but also perhaps realizing that's where the $7,000 bottle of 2000 Chateau Petrus was kept.

Meanwhile, servers dressed as gauchos roved around the restaurant with a dozen kinds of meat on skewers that they carved tableside. This colorful cascade of *carne*—bacon-wrapped filet mignon, rump roast, sausage, barbecue chicken—never stopped coming until diners turned over a personal

Café Bohemia (138 South Clinton Street) was famous for game, including beaver, buffalo and bear. Close to Union Station, it was popular with tourists. *Chicago History Museum.*

disc from green to red, from "bring it on" to *pare* (Portuguese for "enough"). This restaurant closed recently, but Texas de Brazil opened another site at 210 East Illinois Street with the same parade of meat but, sadly, without any wine angels.

The wall of wine and gaucho theme sure beat the mock gothic Eerie World Café that operated at the same location beforehand until 2000. The scariest items in this horror-themed restaurant were the food. And before that, a Jekyll-and-Hyde-themed restaurant briefly occupied the space. Talk about a haunted house.

Other extraordinary eateries in Chicago include Café Bohemia (1936–86), remembered for game, including hippopotamus, moose, elk, bear and more; Schulien's (1881–1999) for tableside magic tricks; Kungsholm (1937–71) for its miniature grand opera puppet show; and Colosimo's (1910–53), where the mob-boss owner was gunned down inside his own restaurant.

Chicago has done peculiar, too. Ronny's Steak Palace featured a mural of Ronald Reagan and Mikhail Gorbachev apparently saluting raw meat; the Old Heidelberg is remembered for yodeling (although never karaoke yodeling); Sally's Stage featured a deafening pipe organ; and at King's Manor, designed like a medieval banquet hall, patrons ate without any utensils while minstrels sang, jesters entertained, friars prayed and boisterous wenches served food, accompanied by unlimited amounts of beer, cider and wine.

One of the most peculiar restaurants was Uncle Tannous at 2626 North Halsted Street, open during the '90s and named after a character on *The Danny Thomas Show*. The Lebanese restaurant with a Moorish interior seemed to be an homage to Thomas, who was Lebanese and partied there regularly. Photos of him adorned the walls. Belly dancing packed the house on Saturday nights. And dancing on the tables was not at all unheard of.

At the other end of the spectrum, some bygone Chicago restaurants were located in remarkable venues. From the mid-1990s to the early 2000s, Beyond Words Café served up a healthy breakfast, luscious lunch buffet and afternoon tea on the ninth floor of the Harold Washington Library Center in a bright, spectacular setting. The Relic House restaurant on Clark Street near Lincoln Park was located in an 1872 house built of debris salvaged from the Chicago Fire. And Palette's, at 1030 North State Street from 1995 until at least 2000, was a work of art, literally. The hand-

The Harold Washington Library Center hosted Beyond Words, a buffet-style restaurant, on the ninth floor of this, the country's largest public library. *Chicago Public Library, Special Collections.*

painted walls, ceilings, columns, tables and chairs provided an attractive setting for the artistically presented food. One mural depicted the history of art. The overall effect suggested a sprawling artist's loft, and painters would occasionally work away at easels.

AIRPLANE AND AIRPORT FOOD

Airplanes and airports are not usually thought of as food destinations, but Chicago delivered some surprises there. In 1961, a Douglas DC-6 headed for O'Hare International Airport was damaged beyond repair on landing. Three years later, the fuselage and wings were hauled to 102 South Cicero Avenue and reassembled into the Sky-Hi Restaurant & Drive-in, which must have been a traffic stopper, as the plane sat on top of the drive-in, seemingly ready to blast off. The plane held about ten tables, each seating four customers. The waitresses wore stewardess uniforms, and the passengers never had to worry about motion sickness.

SKY-HI DRIVE-IN
AND RESTAURANT

Sky-Hi Drive-in put a wrecked DC-6 to novel use. It featured waitresses in stewardess uniforms and an "in-flight menu" of twenty-eight dishes. *Curt Teich Postcard Archives Collection, Newberry Library.*

In addition, Sky-Hi described itself as "all-electric" and boasted of an "in-flight menu" of twenty-eight different dishes, "all prepared by flameless electric cooking equipment." Apparently, this was a reference to microwave ovens, as affordable microwaves were just becoming available in the '60s. The restaurant operated for at least fifteen years.

Through the '40s and '50s, passenger airports were considered novel, and Chicago's airports attracted tourists and locals alike, who came to watch propeller planes and, later, jets take off and land. At the busiest airport in the world in the '40s, Midway Airport's observation deck, perimeter fences and nearby roads attracted large crowds of spectators. Nonetheless, its food accommodations were "primitive, at best," according to Christopher Lynch, author of *Chicago's Midway Airport.* To rectify this, Marshall Field's was asked to open a fine dining and a casual restaurant. In 1948, the company opened the Cloud Room on the second floor in the center of Midway's new terminal and the Blue and Gold Café one floor below. These were Marshall Field's first free-standing restaurants, and both afforded dramatic views of the planes close-up on the tarmac.

The elegant Cloud Room was an immediate success, attracting 1.25 million customers per year in the '50s. This included movie stars Clark Gable, Jack Benny and Jimmy Stewart and hundreds of others as they traveled through. Presidents and sports figures dined there, too, as did locals, who would dress up for the occasion. Despite its prestige, Cloud Room prices were affordable. In 1951, a dinner of roast leg of veal, new parsley potatoes and Danish red cabbage cost $1.80. For Mimi Ferrara, daughter of Midway photographer Mike Rotunno, the most popular items were shrimp cocktail and Mrs. Hering's chicken potpie, the same dish that's still popular at Macy's (then Marshall Field's) Walnut Room. "The Cloud Room was magical," Ferrara said. "Flying was a novelty, so seeing the planes was captivating."

Meanwhile, the Blue and Gold Café catered to travelers in a hurry and local customers on a budget. "With its long, steel lunch counter and checkerboard tile floor, it looked as if it had been taken right out of an Edward Hopper painting," wrote Gayle Soucek in *Marshall Field's: The Store that Helped Build Chicago*.

Judy Anneaux, another Rotunno daughter, recalled having breakfast at the twenty-four-hour Blue and Gold Café with her dad and Harry Truman. "The president surprised us by ordering a shot of bourbon before eating breakfast," Anneaux said.

A large Alexander Calder mobile that had hung in the Cloud Room was later removed and displayed in Marshall Field's stores, including over the women's apparel department of its Northbrook store. (Calder had named the six-piece mobile *Brass in the Sky*, but Marshall Field's renamed it *Flight in Motion*.) Years later, the mobile was donated to the Museum of Contemporary Art.

The two restaurants were large, employing 180 kitchen and wait staff, and Midway boasted that it had the finest dining facilities of any airport in the country. But this was not to last. O'Hare opened to scheduled passenger

From the Cloud Room's second-floor picture windows, patrons could watch planes take off and land, a novelty in the '40s. Marshall Field's ran the restaurant. *Rotunno Family Collection.*

flights in 1955 and quickly eclipsed Midway. The Cloud Room closed in 1962, reflecting the steep decline of air traffic at Midway.

As O'Hare took off, it built its own fine dining restaurant in 1963. Seven Continents provided stunning views of the airfield, especially from coveted window seats. It went all out, with valet parking, fresh-cut flowers, silver water pitchers and exotic foods flown in daily. All the tuxedoed waiters were men recruited from Europe and spoke at least three languages (including English). The luxurious restaurant was located one level above the concourse, on top of the three-story Rotunda Building that connected Terminals 2 and 3.

Ironically, Marshall Field's rival, Carson Pirie Scott, ran Seven Continents. The restaurant's signature dish was chicken Kiev, but it was also known for fresh fish. The food was not on par with that of Chicago's top restaurants, but the setting was original. *Tribune* food critic Phil Vettel assured readers in 1991 that Seven Continents was a "real restaurant...an oasis of civility" in a place characterized by long, crowded corridors full of junk-food vendors. "Give Seven Continents credit for being a far better restaurant than it has to be," he wrote. It continued to be so until closing in the '90s.

CHICAGO'S ALGONQUIN ROUND TABLE

During the '20s, a group of writers, critics and all-around wits lunched daily at a round table in New York's Algonquin Hotel. These tastemakers, including Dorothy Parker, Harold Ross, George Kaufman and Harpo Marx, feasted on wordplay and wisecracks, as well as serious literary analysis. They profoundly influenced literature, drama and criticism nationwide for decades to come.

As a writer, it was gratifying to learn through researching this book that Chicago had its own version of the illustrious Algonquin Round Table. Two, in fact, and both were in full swing at about the same period, perhaps inspired by their New York counterpart.

In 1909, Harriet Brainard married William Vaughn Moody, one of America's leading poets and playwrights. After her husband's untimely death the following year, Moody befriended other poets and authors, according to the marvelous blog Restaurant-ing Through History by Jan Whitaker. In 1920, Moody opened the French restaurant Le Petit Gourmet at 615 North Michigan Avenue and organized poetry nights, giving the admission money to the speakers. *Poetry* magazine founder Harriet Monroe also conducted renowned poetry readings there.

John Drury, in his comprehensive 1931 guidebook *Dining in Chicago*, wrote that Le Petit Gourmet "has always been popular among writers" and noted that it played a big role in introducing Chicago to the work of Carl Sandburg, Robert Frost, Amy Lowe, Edgar Lee Masters and many other notable poets. Moody herself got the writing bug and penned the somewhat successful *Mrs. William Vaughn Moody's Cookbook*.

Some of the authors who rubbed shoulders at Le Petit Gourmet also gathered at Schlogl's Restaurant & Saloon at 37 North Wells Street, which opened in 1879. At a round table in a corner of this German restaurant, a loose group of newspaper reporters and literary luminaries gathered once a week. They included Sandburg, Masters, Sherwood Anderson, Ben Hecht, John T. McCutcheon, Theodore Dreiser, Henry Justin Smith and many others.

Occasionally, this group, which gathered for inspiration as well as the food, got rowdy. Smith relates in his book *Chicago's Left Bank* that he and Hecht sawed off the legs of the chair upon which visiting English author Hugh

Schlogl's round table was Chicago's answer to New York's Algonquin Round Table. From the 1920s to the '50s, it attracted leading authors, poets, critics and journalists. *Chicago History Museum.*

Walpole was to sit. Hecht later admitted that stitches had been required to mend the damage.

The origin of Schlogl's round table are unclear, but one story goes like this. In 1916, Henry Blackman Sell, a book lover and former furniture salesman, promised the *Chicago Daily News* that its reporters could eat at Schlogl's for free if the paper would hire him as editor of its new book-review section. Sell became the editor, but it's unclear whether anyone ate for free at Schlogl's as a result. For a time, however, newspaper artists and writers whose work appeared in print that day ate at Schlogl's for free.

"Naturally, the 'Who's Who' of the American literary world would not come here unless the cuisine were such as to meet the approval of fastidious men of letters," Drury wrote. "This place serves food that the most cosmopolitan of epicures would revel in. The Stewed Chicken a la Schlogl can be gotten nowhere else....There is also savory Wiener Schnitzel and Hasenpfeffer, roast young duck, and bouillabaisse. The Schlogl pancake is deserving of a chapter to itself....You haven't dined in Chicago unless you've eaten at least once in this historic restaurant."

Schlogl's reputation for literary excellence was partly fueled by Richard Schneider, a waiter there who collected autographs of distinguished writers. To be asked to sign Schneider's autograph book "was practically an assurance of fame," the *Tribune* wrote in 1950, near the date this esteemed restaurant closed.

Illinois is the Land of Lincoln, and many Chicago establishments—from the reviled Lincoln Towing to the highly regarded Abraham Lincoln Elementary School—make reference to the revered sixteenth president. Unsurprisingly, restaurants also engaged in this practice. The most notable one was the Lincoln Restaurant at 4008 North Lincoln Avenue. Greek immigrant John Athans opened this 250-seat restaurant in 1970 and named it Lincoln simply because he liked the president. "He did a lot of good things for the country," Athans told the *Tribune* in 1995, just after replacing a small black-and-white sign with a huge red, white and blue one of a quizzical Lincoln that could be seen from up and down the street. Pictures and busts of Lincoln decorated the inside, which carried a Civil War theme. It was a blow to the neighborhood when this restaurant closed abruptly in 2013.

CHAPTER 2

Early Restaurants

T rue to its reputation as a crossroads, Chicago's first restaurants were in taverns and inns that served travelers. Initially, those travelers arrived via waterways, so eating, drinking and hostelry were first offered along the Chicago River, starting at Wolf's Point. Wolf Point Tavern, the first in 1828, was followed by the Eagle Exchange Tavern in 1829 and the Sauganash Hotel in 1831. Miller House and Caldwell's Tavern followed soon thereafter.

These taverns and inns were rough-and-tumble places. They provided food in a welcoming, even festive environment, but the fare was bleak and heavy on salt pork, bread, corn, potatoes and stews. Although plentiful, given the abundance of fish, game and wild berries, the simple, basic food was "indifferently cooked and still more (indifferently) served," according to Patrick Shirreff, who passed through in 1833. "The table had no charms to the epicure," another traveler, Joseph Balestier, wrote a few years later.

Edwin Gale visited riverside taverns in the 1830s, and his son said the food was so plentiful "that it rendered us oblivious to chipped dishes, flies buzzing, tangled in the butter, creeping beetles and the music of mosquito bands." Of course, alcohol, companionship and news were as much a draw at these taverns and inns as was the food.

Things began to change when the lavish Lake House, Chicago's first luxury hotel, opened in 1835—before the city even incorporated. The impressive three-story brick building stood on the north side of the river on what was then the lakefront, where the Wrigley Building stands today.

Lake House, Chicago's first luxury hotel, opened in 1835 near the river and lake. Its restaurant introduced elegance and fine food—for the wealthy. *Chicago History Museum.*

Lake House quickly became the center of social and political life, at least for the well-heeled.

The hotel was "superiour...excellent...Elysium," in the words of James Buckingham, a sophisticated British visitor in 1840. Its restaurant introduced the coarse diners of this hardscrabble town to tablecloths, napkins, printed menus—even toothpicks. It claimed in 1838 to have the first restaurant in Chicago to serve live oysters, transported from New England by sleigh. Travelers and Chicagoans could now "indulge in all the luxuries of the east," Balestier wrote.

Other hotels followed Lake House's example and included excellent restaurants. They employed French chefs, offered entertainment and went overboard to outdo each. Today, Chicagoans are less likely to go to hotel restaurants for a night out, but for the city's first eighty years or so, fine restaurants in opulent hotels dominated destination dining.

STAND-ALONE RESTAURANTS

Early on, many hotels followed the so-called American Plan, which charged guests for their meals along with their room. Likewise, boardinghouses, where less well-to-do travelers and newly arrived settlers typically stayed, included meals with the cost of their lodging. These practices provided a disincentive for chefs and entrepreneurs to open stand-alone restaurants. According to the *Chicago Food Encyclopedia*, it was not until 1844 that Chicago got its first free-standing restaurant, the Exchange Coffee House. Three years later, there were still only nine free-standing restaurants in Chicago.

This situation persisted until the 1870s, by which time the Civil War had made Chicago prosperous and left locals with a lot more money to spend eating out. Hotels gradually switched to the European Plan, which did not charge guests for meals as part of their stay, and this also encouraged stand-alone restaurants.

In addition, by the 1870s, Chicago was the undisputed rail center of the country. Cross-country travelers had to change trains here to continue their

Rudimentary restaurants and boardinghouses were rough places, patronized primarily by men. Food was plentiful, but manners were scarce. *Chicago History Museum.*

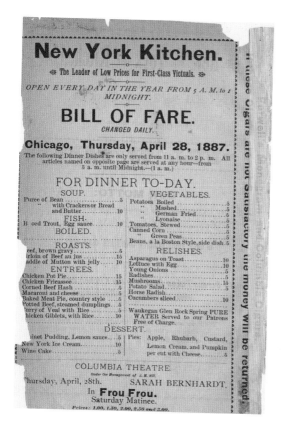

New York Kitchen.

◈ The Leader of Low Prices for First-Class Victuals. ◈

OPEN EVERY DAY IN THE YEAR FROM 5 A. M. to 1 MIDNIGHT.

BILL OF FARE.

CHANGED DAILY.

Chicago, Thursday, April 28, 1887.

The following Dinner Dishes are only served from 11 a. m. to 2 p. m. All articles named on opposite page are served at any hour—from 5 a. m. until Midnight.—(1 a. m.)

FOR DINNER TO-DAY.

SOUP.	VEGETABLES.
Puree of Bean 5	Potatoes Boiled 5
" with Crackers or Bread and Butter............10	" Mashed..................5
FISH.	" German Fried..........5
B oed Trout, Egg sauce.........10	" Lyonaise................5
BOILED.	Tomatoes, Stewed...........5
	Canned Corn...............5
ROASTS.	" Green Peas.............5
eef, brown gravy.............5	Beans, a la Boston Style, side dish .5
irloin of Beef au jus 15	RELISHES.
addle of Mutton with jelly... 10	Asparagus on Toast.............10
ENTREES.	Lettuce with Egg.............10
Chicken Pot Pie.............15	Young Onions 5
Chicken Fricassee............15	Radishes.....................5
Corned Beef Hash 5	Mushrooms...................15
Macaroni and cheese 5	Potato Salad.................5
Baked Meat Pie, country style 5	Horse Radish.................5
Potted Beef, steamed dumplings...5	Cucumbers sliced 10
urry of Veal with Rice 5	
hicken Giblets, with Rice.......10	Waukegan Glen Rock Spring PURE WATER Served to our Patrons Free of Charge.
DESSERT.	
lnet Pudding, Lemon sauce....5	Pies: Apple, Rhubarb, Custard,
New York Ice Cream..............10	Lemon Cream, and Pumpkin
Wine Cake....................5	per cut with Cheese.........5

COLUMBIA THEATRE.

Under the Management of J. H. Hill.

hursday, April, 28th. SARAH BERNHARDT.

In **Frou Frou.**
Saturday Matinee.

Prices: 1.00, 1.50, 2.00, 2.50 and 3.00.

The New York Kitchen on Clark Street in 1887 felt it necessary to say on its menu, "No scraps taken back into the kitchen and cooked over." *Chicago History Museum.*

journey, something that typically involved an overnight stay or a layover of at least a few hours. Many restaurants were created to serve these train travelers looking for a meal.

Fred Harvey recognized this business opportunity. Beginning in 1875, he opened more than eighty Harvey House restaurants along railroad lines in the West. This constituted the first restaurant chain in the United States and grew to include restaurants in Chicago, such as one in Union Station. The chain's specially trained waitresses, known as Harvey Girls, were required to be young, attractive, single, white and well educated. They provided the Harvey Houses with "class and civility," as portrayed by Judy Garland in the 1946 film *The Harvey Girls*. The chain formed a partnership with the Santa Fe Railway that endured from 1878 until the mid-1980s. If the Harvey name sounds familiar, that's because from 1959 until 1975, Fred Harvey Restaurants served Illinois Tollway oases (including the O'Hare Oasis) on bridges that spanned the highways.

RAILROAD CUSTOMERS

Most early Chicago restaurants—whether in hotels or stand-alone—that catered to travelers were located near train stations. Virtually all of them have disappeared with the decline of intercity passenger train travel, starting in the '50s. One restaurant originally aimed squarely at rail passengers that still survives is Lou Mitchell's. It opened in 1923 at 565 West Jackson Boulevard, just a stone's throw from Union Station. Today, many patrons of this legendary restaurant juggle suitcases or backpacks as they take in a meal and a dose of history between trains.

One of the most treasured restaurants popular with train travelers was Blackie's at Polk and Clark Streets, about one block from both the Dearborn and LaSalle Street Stations. When Alex DeMilio decided to open a restaurant in 1939, his friend and big-band leader Jimmy Dorsey promised to help attract celebrity customers traveling through Chicago—as long as DeMilio gave a man nicknamed "Blackie" a job. DeMilio not only complied but even named the place after him. Dorsey carried through with his promise, and Blackie's became a hot spot for the likes of Tony Bennett, Elizabeth Taylor and Chico Marx.

Blackie's survived for seventy-eight colorful years. "Back when the South Loop was a seedy vice district, bookies ran numbers from Blackie's second floor," said Jeffrey Thomas, DeMilio's grandson. "Judges played cards in the basement, and cops were on the take, collecting a weekly drop."

"Back in the day, when the bar 'closed' it didn't close," Thomas added. "We just locked the door and pulled the curtains."

Thomas, who grew up in the restaurant and started working there in 1977, kept the place running until 2017. "I couldn't stand working sixty hours a week anymore, and no one else in the family wanted to continue it," he lamented.

CHAPTER 3

Quick Food, Lunch Bunch

s Chicago grew in population and size during the last three decades
of the nineteenth century, locals became increasingly likely to eat at
restaurants, especially for their midday meal. Those with jobs, whether
working class or white collar, were less likely than in the past to return
home for lunch because their jobs tended to be farther from home than
before. In addition, the Industrial Age shortened their lunch breaks to sixty
minutes, thirty minutes or less. And the Industrial Age introduced shiftwork,
which created the need for on-the-job meals twenty-four hours a day.

All of these factors led to the development of meal wagons that traveled
to factories and office buildings around the clock. They also contributed to
a restaurant boom, in particular with restaurants that specialized in cheap
food and speedy service. Yes, before there was fast food, there was quick
food. It was available in a number of different settings: lunchrooms, coffee
shops, sandwich shops, cafeterias and the like—all catering to the growing
need for quick, convenient, inexpensive midday (or midnight) meals.

The early food carts and lunch wagons that plied the streets and sidewalks
sold such things as fruit, popcorn and peanuts. Soon these rolling providers
added cooking gear to offer roasted corn, sausage, eggs, fried chicken and
other simple prepared foods. Predictably, the presence of such purveyors
irritated established restaurants, which were burdened with more overhead.
Also, many people feared food carts and wagons were unsafe and unsanitary.
As a result, regulations were developed to restrict the number and variety
of food carts and lunch wagons. To counter these pressures, some of these

The first Thompson's opened in 1891. By 1916, when this photo was taken, it was running one of the largest quick-food cafeteria chains in the country. *Chicago History Museum.*

roving eateries locked their wheels and set up shop in stationary, semi-permanent locations. Others opened true restaurants. Both reactions led to more quick-food restaurants.

Early on, such rudimentary, unpretentious quick-food restaurants offered soups and sandwiches, coffee and tea but not much in the way of ambiance. A guidebook of the day described the experience of eating at one such restaurant thus: "You sit on a stool, hat on, people waiting for your seat, no napkin but quick service." The menu listed "nothing that required special preparation," the guidebook added. Saloons also helped fill the need for quick meals, and many offered free food with the purchase of an alcoholic beverage, or two.

The saloons and rudimentary restaurants did not welcome women, especially if they were not accompanied by a man. For women of leisure, department stores began offering food, starting with Marshall Field's in 1890 with a modest tearoom on the third floor of its downtown store. Marshall Field's claimed the tearoom was the world's first restaurant in a department store. In any event, it encouraged female customers to continue shopping rather than return home for a meal. The tearoom was such a hit that Marshall Field's added many more restaurants. Other downtown department stores, which at their peak numbered eight on State Street alone, followed suit. Of these department stores, only Marshall Field's successor, Macy's, remains, and it continues to run restaurants, the most famous of which is Marshall Field's historic Walnut Room.

Tearooms, ice cream shops, "dairy lunchrooms" and other establishments offered additional places for women to eat. In 1880, for example, Herman H. Kohlsaat opened a lunch counter as part of a bakery with which he was affiliated. It was successful, so he opened more "bakery counters," especially downtown.

There were so many lunch places downtown that the area around Clark and Madison Streets became known as "toothpick alley."

B/G Foods ran a popular string of sandwich shops. Looking southeast from Rush and Oak Streets, the Drake Hotel and Palmolive Building stand out. *Ryerson, Burnham Archives, Art Institute of Chicago.*

This "cheap eats" frenzy contributed to the development of chain restaurants downtown and, less so, in busy shopping districts outside the Loop. Homegrown chains, whether cafeterias or sandwich shops, included Pixley & Ehlers and B/G Foods. The former, often described as "greasy spoons," attracted customers mainly because they seemed to be open at all hours and their food was inexpensive. Chicago's earliest lunchroom chains "set a benchmark for plentiful food, fast service, contemporary décor and modest prices," wrote Eric Bronsky and Neal Samors in their comprehensive book *Chicago's Classic Restaurants*.

Meanwhile, quick-food chains from out of town opened in Chicago, including Waldorf Lunch out of Boston and Childs Unique Dairy Lunch out of New York, the latter known for its white-tiled walls that were meant to project a clean image.

THOMPSON'S CAFETERIAS

The John R. Thompson Co., perhaps the most important early quick-food chain in Chicago, started in 1891 on State Street and rapidly opened additional outlets. It ran "one-arm" lunchrooms, so called because they were furnished with wood chairs that had a small working surface on one side, like an old-fashioned school desk, only in this case the arm was used to hold a meal rather than a notebook, and the small round opening on the arm was for a coffee mug—an early cup holder!—rather than for an inkwell.

Thompson's grew into a very successful chain. It was run on a "scientific" basis, emphasizing speed, nutrition, efficiency and quality, all at a low price. Its lunchrooms were typically attractive but stark, laid out in a long line, perpendicular to the street. To maximize speed during the sporadic rush of customers, employees served customers along an unusual feature: a cafeteria line.

Today's fast-food offerings of hamburgers, fries and carbonated drinks were not on Thompson's menu. Instead, patrons found somewhat more healthy sandwiches, typically made of cheese, ham, tongue or eggs, as well as soup, salad, milk, fresh fruit and dessert, such as pies and pastries. A 1911 advertisement claimed that lunch "won't leave you logy, lazy and dull this afternoon."

By 1921, Thompson's had expanded to Canada and New York, with a total of 109 restaurants, 49 of which were in Chicago. This made it one of

Above: Thompson's exemplified cleanliness and speed. This "one-arm" lunchroom at 528 North Clark Street was furnished with chairs that had an arm from which to eat. *Chicago History Museum.*

Below: This Thompson's was in the company's commissary at 350 North Clark Street. The building still stands, and a big terra-cotta T is visible above the entrance. *Krambles-Peterson Archive.*

the country's largest chains. Over the years, Thompson's absorbed other Chicago restaurants, including Henrici's, a formal, storied restaurant, and Raklios', another quick-food chain. In the '50s, Thompson's dropped its original restaurant design in favor of other concepts, including the Red Balloon Coffee houses and Holloway House cafeterias.

TOFFENETTI-TRIANGLE RESTAURANTS

In 1914, Austrian immigrant Dario Toffenetti opened the Triangle, a small restaurant near Clark and Randolph Streets. Besides running an efficient, affordable restaurant, he implemented new advertising and marketing techniques—while learning them in night school at Northwestern University's School of Commerce. At his restaurants, Toffenetti promoted

Dario Toffenetti opened this restaurant at 57 West Randolph Street in the early 1900s and mastered efficient, streamlined service, as well as marketing and promotion. *University of Illinois at Chicago Library.*

Toffenetti's forty-foot-long "Liquid Lifetime" fountain at 119 South Clark Street in the mid-1930s. *Chicago History Museum.*

ham, but not just any ham. It was "Roasted Sugar Cured Ham from Oscar Mayer's." He claimed that his spaghetti sauce had been discovered "among the ruins of the ancient castle of the count of Bonpensler in Bologna." And he boasted the best potatoes from Idaho, selling so many that he got an exceptional discount. (This presaged McDonald's current dominance of the Idaho potato crop.)

By 1937, there were six Toffenetti-Triangle restaurants in the Loop, all moderately priced, serving large portions and guaranteed, by the founder himself, to please. A progressive force in the industry, Toffenetti employed large plate-glass windows in the front of his restaurants, pioneered the idea of an open kitchen and advertised that all his restaurants were spanking clean. Toffenetti's success drove him to expand to New York, where he operated a restaurant in Times Square from 1940 to 1968. His Chicago restaurants lasted until the early '80s.

OTHER CHAINS AND LUNCH COUNTERS

Drugstores were also influential in developing fast food. Since the early 1800s, pharmacies had typically included a soda fountain because carbonated water was considered medicinal. As druggists added flavored syrups and later ice cream to the effervescent water, soda fountains became ornate. They were extremely profitable, but only during warm months. To extend the service and allow soda fountains to operate year-round, some pharmacies added sandwiches, hot food and pastries—and the lunch counter was born. In one telling case, Charles Walgreen opened his first drugstore on Cottage Grove Boulevard near Bowen Avenue in 1901. It included a soda fountain, and after a few years, Walgreen added food cooked by his wife, Myrtle. The experiment thrived, and twenty years later, a Walgreen's "soda jerk" invented the malted milkshake, further popularizing lunch counters.

In the early twentieth century, John Raklios, a Greek immigrant who began his career by peddling fruit in the street, launched a chain of "luncheonettes." These restaurants were a cut above mere lunch counters, offering more hot food and a broader menu. Also, they were less conventional than traditional restaurants and therefore easier to finance, open and operate. By 1923, Chicagoland sported at least seventeen Raklios' luncheonettes.

Another chain worth mentioning is Faber Cafeterias, of which there were once twenty-two in Chicago, including ones in the Richard J. Daley Center, Pittsfield Building and Riverside Plaza. When the last one closed in 1999, the *Tribune* called them "nondescript…but convenient." Another chain, Harding's, had up to a dozen restaurants concentrated downtown during the '40s. Famous for corned beef and cabbage, its restaurants were characterized by checkerboard floors and long, deep counters, with tables along the side. One Harding's stood out: the Colonial Room on the second floor at 21 South Wabash Avenue, where servers were dressed in costumes from colonial days.

The Harding's, Thompson's, Harvey Houses and other chains standardized the retailing of quick, cheap food sold in a clean, open setting, thereby helping to develop the modern fast-food model. In so doing, they pushed out many of Chicago's mom-and-pop lunchrooms, some of which were run by first- and second-generation immigrants.

Today, for a taste of that quick, affordable cafeteria, lunch counter or luncheonette that one might have experienced at Raklios' or Toffenetti's, visit Moon's Sandwich Shop (16 South Western Avenue) or Valois Restaurant (1518 East Fifty-Third Street). Valois's open kitchen and motto, "See your

Shoub's, a bare-bones lunchroom at 500 South Wells Street, in 1940. A filling meal cost thirty cents. *Eric Bronsky.*

food," speak to the openness and cleanliness these early twentieth-century quick-food restaurants strove to project. Opened in 1921, "The Valoyz" (as locals pronounce it) is a treasured Hyde Park institution with a loyal, diverse following. Another holdover cafeteria-style restaurant, Manny's Coffee Shop & Deli (1141 South Jefferson Street), is also worth a visit. Founded in 1942, it dishes out large portions at affordable prices in a no-frills, efficient manner.

CHAPTER 4

Hotel Restaurants

rand "palace" hotels, with restaurants fit for royalty, were appearing on the East Coast in the 1820s. The idea caught on quickly in burgeoning Chicago with the construction of the elegant Lake House in 1835, two years before the city even incorporated. It housed an elegant (for its time) restaurant that put Chicago on the fine dining map early in its history. Ever since, Windy City luxury hotels have enticed travelers and locals with delicious food served stylishly, even ostentatiously. Hotel restaurants catered to the high end of the market. Travelers were willing to pay for good food to ease what was typically an arduous journey, and local diners looked to hotel restaurants for a delicious meal and an exceptional dining experience.

The first Tremont House, at the northwest corner of Lake and Dearborn Streets, followed in the Lake House's tasteful path. Unfortunately, little is known about this highly regarded hotel since it burned down three years later. Fire also destroyed the second rendition, but the third Tremont House, built in 1850, excelled and was regarded as the premier hotel in all of what was then considered "the West."

Increasingly, hotels and their inviting restaurants helped to position Chicago as a way station for travelers. Soon, especially with the growing dominance of rail transportation, the city became the most popular stopover town in the world.

The World's Columbian Exposition of 1893 stimulated the development of hotels and their restaurants. For instance, two Belgian brothers came to

The Palmer House set a high standard for hotel restaurants. The Victorian Room in the 1880s proved that the city had recovered from the Chicago Fire. *Chicago History Museum.*

Chicago to run a café at the fair. Since it went well, they stayed and opened the DeJonghe Hotel and Restaurant at 12 East Monroe Street in 1899. It closed in 1923 due to Prohibition-related liquor violations, but its signature dish, Shrimp DeJonghe, lives on: shrimp baked with garlic, onions, breadcrumbs and lots of butter. This restaurant also popularized escargot in Chicago.

The Sherman House was founded in 1836 by the son of Civil War general William Tecumseh Sherman and survived, albeit with multiple rebuilds, all the way until 1973! Its fourth and last iteration, a magnificent building at 150 West Randolph Street, was razed to make room for the James R. Thompson Center. Hotel Sherman (as it became known) included the legendary College Inn, one of Chicago's most famous restaurants. Its fancy food was so good that it led to a large line of College Inn branded products, and its broths and stocks are sold to this day.

Even more memorable than the College Inn's food was its entertainment. Near the end of the 1800s, the restaurant began to offer live music and dancing. Later, it was the first place many Chicagoans heard jazz. In 1914,

Left: Hotels competed vigorously for diners. Both the Sherman House and Morrison Hotel staged ice shows on the dance floors of their restaurants. *Eric Bronsky.*

Right: Oysters were popular by 1875, when the Wilson (later Boston) Oyster House opened. The shellfish came in by train from the East Coast. *Chicago History Museum.*

a night of dinner and dancing at the College Inn cost a whopping $1.50 per person, but that included an astonishing floor show: skaters performing on a miniature rink of real ice. The ice show was so successful that restaurants and nightclubs around the country copied the idea. From the '30s to the '40s, the restaurant hosted big-name groups, such as Tommy Dorsey and Cab Calloway. Like many other bygone hotel restaurants, the College Inn broadcast its entertainment on the radio for years. Hotel Sherman and the College Inn closed in 1973.

One place to pick up on the ice-skating idea was the Morrison Hotel, a crosstown rival of the Sherman House located at the corner of Clark and Madison Streets. It installed a large rink on the dance floor of its spectacular Terrace Garden on the first floor of the hotel. Billed as "Chicago's Wonder Restaurant," the Terrace Garden served lavish meals and featured hundreds of tables that were terraced around a huge dance floor.

The Morrison Hotel had roots back to 1838, but this, the last iteration of the hotel, was constructed in pieces from 1915 to 1937. Along the way, it also housed the Boston Oyster House in its basement, the restaurant/nightclub Carousel in the Sky on its forty-sixth floor and, in between, The Grill, an informal pub with a Dutch-inspired décor. The building was razed in 1965 to make way for the First National Bank Building.

HOTELING THROUGH HISTORY

The Gilded Age was not as opulent in Chicago as it was in New York, but during the 1880s and 1890s, many hotel restaurants fought to outdo one another with plush settings and impressive menus. Many wealthy locals took up residence in these opulent hotels, enticed by the fine food, comfortable living quarters and pretentious addresses.

The Bismarck Hotel, built in 1894 at 171 West Randolph Street, was remarkable in many ways. The Eitel brothers, the hotel's high-profile founders, sought and gained permission to use the name for their hotel from German chancellor Otto von Bismarck. During World War I, they regretted that choice and changed the name to Randolph. After the war, they changed it back to Bismarck, but either way, it was known for its excellent restaurants.

The original Bismarck was razed and rebuilt in 1926, with several top-quality restaurants, including the elegant Walnut Room (not the one at Marshall Field's) and the chic, Art Deco Green Emerald Room. Other restaurants came and went at the Bismarck, as the hotel remodeled and reconfigured its spaces. In the '60s, one could dine there in the Swiss Chalet Room on schnitzel Emmenthal, spaetzle Geschnetzeltes and Edelweiss torte. The Bismarck closed in 1996 and was reopened two years later as the Hotel Allegro, with beautifully restored original features.

Chicago's economic boom and population growth of the Roaring Twenties coupled with the city's rising appeal as a good place to meet or host a convention led to a building boom in restaurants and hotels. This led to a golden age for Chicago hotel restaurants, a time when they offered entertainment and before jet travel replaced train travel and automobiles assured diners more dining choices.

The current Palmer House, Chicago's best-known hotel of all time, was built in 1925 and held fantastic floor shows in its legendary Empire Room. This strikingly elegant restaurant, with crystal chandeliers and twenty-four-karat-gold-leaf ornamentation, was famous for welcoming movie, radio and television personalities. Meanwhile, the huge Stevens Hotel (now Hilton

Left: German immigrants Robert and Max Eitel ran several successful restaurants, including the Old Heidelberg and one in their Bismarck Hotel. *Chicago History Museum.*

Below: The beloved Edgewater Beach Hotel offered food and entertainment at the Colonnade (pictured here), Marine Dining and Polynesian Rooms. *Author's collection.*

Chicago) opened in 1927 and held entertaining floor shows in its renowned Boulevard Room restaurant. The historic Congress Hotel had its Pompeiian Room, with a large ground-level fountain that seemed to invite revelers to take a dip every New Year's Eve. And the storied Blackstone, where politicians cut deals over breakfast, lunch and dinner, had its Café Bonaparte.

Chicago's most fondly remembered bygone hotel would have to be the "sunrise-yellow" Edgewater Beach Hotel at Berwyn Avenue and Lake Michigan. It opened in 1916 and developed into a luxurious, multi-building resort, complete with several restaurants, a nine-hole putting golf course and seaplane service to downtown. The food in the fabulous Marine Dining Room, with its sunken floor, was expensive but exquisite—from the beluga caviar canapes to the prime rib to the caramel-nut layer cake. The hotel's Yacht Club offered snacks and exotic cocktails and had canvas walls that would move up and down at the toss of a switch to simulate sailing.

Music and entertainment were a central part of the restaurants' appeal. In the winter or during bad weather, bands played inside, but when the weather was nice, they played outside on the marble-tiled Beach Walk alongside the hotel's 1,200-foot private beach. All the top bands, like Benny Goodman, Artie Shaw and Glenn Miller, performed there. For years, the music was broadcast nationally over NBC stations and locally over WEBH, the resort's own radio station. Regular diners included the rich and famous, like Cary Grant, Babe Ruth and more than one U.S. president. And the hotel's restaurants witnessed countless conventions, weddings, bar mitzvahs and proms.

Things were definitely cooler by the lake, but this enchanted waterfront resort was too good to last. At some point, the fine dining Marine Dining Room was replaced by the less classy Polynesian Room, which some longtime employees disdainfully referred to as a "chop suey joint." Starting in 1951, Lake Shore Drive was extended through the property, cutting the hotel off from its prized namesake lakefront. After that, things declined, and the resort closed in 1967. The 1928 "sunset-pink" Edgewater Beach Apartments is all that's left of the complex.

Evidence of the Tip Top Tap, another favorite hotel restaurant that bit the dust, can still be seen on top of the Warwick Allerton Hotel at 701 North Michigan Avenue. When the Allerton opened in 1924, it towered

A menu cover from the stunning Empire Room. Most major hotels had elegant restaurants that catered to local residents, as well as hotel guests. *Chicago History Museum.*

over the relatively sedate area, characterized by stately nineteenth-century townhouses. The building's height gave prominence to its large distinctive sign adverting the Tip Top Tap, a bar/restaurant on the twenty-third floor. The restaurant, later called the Cloud Room, is remembered less for its food and more as the site of Don McNeill's *Breakfast Club*, a radio program broadcast live from the restaurant for two hours, Monday through Friday, from 1933 to 1968.

Millions of people loved the *Breakfast Club*, which was heard on up to four hundred stations. The show was pure unabashed corn, but listeners related to its down-to-earth Midwestern friendliness. Most remarkably, every fifteen minutes McNeil would announce a "Call to Breakfast" that invited listeners to "march around the breakfast table." In 1968, the building, along with its sign, was designated a Chicago landmark, so they're both here to stay. A recent $40 million tiptop-to-bottom renovation of the hotel included converting the Cloud Room into a stunning meeting space for private events and rechristening it the Tip Top Tap Ballroom.

CHAPTER 5

Fine Dining

H otels may have had a head start on fine dining in Chicago, but stand-alone restaurants gradually caught up, established solid reputations and attracted well-to-do customers. One of the most prominent and best remembered fine dining restaurants was Henrici's, opened in 1868 as a Viennese pastry shop in the theater district. Despite its motto, "All you can eat for a quarter," Henrici's was elegant and served exquisite pastries. After moves caused by the Chicago Fire and other issues, Henrici in 1893 opened a new restaurant at 71 West Randolph Street, expanded its menu and went high-end.

HENRICI'S

The huge restaurant seated five hundred patrons and was modeled after the grand dining halls of Austria. Adorned with stained-glass windows and original oil paintings, the dark formal Henrici's typified old Chicago and became immensely popular. It introduced many Chicagoans to European dishes, such as finnan haddie, chicken croquettes and pickled lamb's tongue, all the while emphasizing its delicious pastries, witnessed by a large cake counter prominently positioned near the entrance. Long before Greek restaurants started to serve flaming saganaki, Henrici's wowed diners with flaming pancakes rolled around apples or blueberries. And its front table

Henrici's, Chicago's longest-lasting (1868–1962) fine dining restaurant, was characterized by dignity, decorum and delicious food. *Chicago History Museum.*

"was a resting place for the elbows of celebrities at a time when The Pump Room's Booth No. 1 wasn't even a twinkle in an architect's eye," wrote the *Tribune* years later.

Henrici's eschewed the trend to offer music or entertainment, promising "no orchestral din." The goal was to allow patrons to enjoy fine food and engaging conversation in a dignified setting.

In 1929, the Thompson's cafeteria chain acquired Henrici's but wisely kept the legendary restaurant's successful approach and menu. Incredibly, Henrici's managed to survive almost a century before it was demolished in 1962 to make way for the Civic (now Richard J. Daley) Center. During its last three days, Henrici's served more than twenty-two thousand nostalgic patrons, many of whom wore costumes from the 1890s for their last meal at the celebrated establishment. The restaurant's paintings and panels were carefully removed in the hope that Henrici's would rise again. (We're still waiting.)

Another piece of art connected with Henrici's also appears to be lost. It was created by Chicago artist Felix Ruvolo for a restaurant on the first floor of the Merchandise Mart. It's not known when Henrici's opened this branch, but it was remodeled starting in 1947. Patrick Steffes detailed the artwork in an entry on Forgotten Chicago's authoritative, richly illustrated

Henrici's was torn down to make way for the Civic (now Richard J. Daley) Center. On its last day, customers donned costumes from the 1890s. *Eric Bronsky.*

website, writing that it featured a brilliant, luminescent mural that glowed under a black light. Architect and designer James Eppenstein led the remodeling, and his "modernist style included custom furniture, extensive use of glass and deluxe materials, and a serpentine arrangement of the bar and seating area…that were in stark contrast to the very formal arrangement seen at [Henrici's] Loop location," Steffes wrote. "The results of this high-profile restaurant and bar commission in what was then the world's largest commercial building were spectacular."

TIP TOP INN

In 1884, the Pullman Building was completed at the southwest corner of Adams Street and Michigan Avenue. In addition to housing the offices of the Pullman Palace Car Company, this imposing edifice devoted the seventh, eighth and ninth floors to residences for bachelors and small families "who wish to avoid the cares of housekeeping," as the company put it. No cooking was allowed in these small apartments, so the Albion restaurant was built on the ninth floor to serve these residents. As the apartments were gradually converted into offices, however, the restaurant was reoriented toward the public. In 1893 or 1894, Adolph Hieronymus assumed management of Albion and renamed it the Tip Top Inn (not to be confused with the Tip Top Tap, later located in the Allerton Hotel).

The Tip Top Inn was oddly configured, with at least five dining rooms. Over the years, these rooms were decorated in a dizzying array of themes, including colonial, a kindergarten, the Charles Dickens Corner and Flemish, French and Italian décors. The most unusual was the Whist Room, decorated with enlarged playing cards. Hearts, spades, diamonds and clubs decorated the menus, china and lanterns.

The Tip Top Inn's fanciful approach to decorating must have worked because the restaurant attracted "everyone who's anyone," as newspapers put it, everyone from Yankee Doodle Dandy (George Cohan) to Diamond Jim Brady; Shoeless Joe Jackson to Babe Ruth; J.P. Morgan to Thomas Edison. Such luminaries may have been attracted by the creative cooking, manifested by a 1929 ad that said, "For a revelation in food flavor, try one of our 108 Original Tip Top Inn creations…high up where it's cool and comfortable" (a big draw before air conditioning). These food innovations included Imperial Fruit Salad, Stuffed Whitefish with Crabmeat, Suzettes Tip Top, and Milk-fed Chicken, fried Arkansas-style (whatever that was). And the food was served in a distinctively proper fashion. The Tip Top Inn had "a halo of dignity about it," wrote a former employee.

At some point, Hieronymus added another restaurant in the building, the Black Cat Inn, noted for its unusual practice of hiring black waitresses. This may have been intended to reflect the practice of hiring African American male waiters at the Tip Top Inn—itself an outgrowth of Pullman's practice of hiring African American men as porters on its palatial railcars.

Hit hard by the limitations of Prohibition, the Tip Top Inn closed in 1931. In 2016, a new restaurant at 1204 North State Street claimed the name and heritage of the original Tip Top Inn. It closed within a year, attesting to the difficulty of succeeding as the knockoff of a restaurant, no matter how popular the original one was.

KINSLEY'S

Another early fine dining standout was Kinsley's, opened in 1885 at 105 West Adams Street in a four-story Moorish-style building. Some called this expensive place Chicago's answer to Manhattan's Delmonico's, widely regarded as the country's finest white-tablecloth restaurant. Kinsley's stature cannot be overstated. It inaugurated the World's Columbian Exposition with a banquet for some one hundred dignitaries, including twenty-seven governors, four Supreme Court justices, seventeen ministers of foreign governments, nine U.S. cabinet members, Vice President Adlai E. Stevenson I and former president Rutherford B. Hayes.

The restaurant's pioneering founder, Herbert Kinsley, took positions on the issues of race and tipping that were at odds with many of his peers, according to the blog Restaurant-ing Through History. For example, he was always ready to hire African American waiters and to serve African American customers, rare positions in the 1880s. And Kinsley declared tipping a reasonable system of remuneration that encouraged good service. (Tipping had been imported from Europe in the 1840s, but Americans then considered it unegalitarian and demeaning to the recipient.)

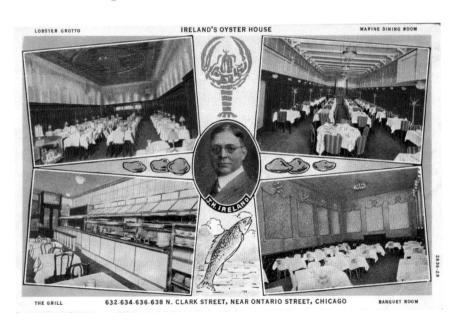

Ireland's opened in 1900, serving "every conceivable form of deep-sea delicacy," quite a novelty at the time. And yet it's remembered as relatively affordable. *Author's collection.*

When Kinsley's closed in 1905, "every table was filled," the *Tribune* recalled years later. "And when the guests left, all the silver service and a lot of the best china went with them!"

OYSTER MANIA

Starting in the 1850s, oysters were all the rage nationwide, and an enormous number were devoured in Chicago. The interest in oysters was driven by a super abundance of the bivalve on the coasts, where supplies seemed inexhaustible. It may also have been influenced by the legend and lore surrounding these tasty gifts of the sea. The Roman author Pliny the Elder called them "the pleasure of the table." The British Empire regarded the indolent mollusk one of the jewels in its crown. And Casanova was said to consume fifty a day, which contributed to the oyster's reputation as an aphrodisiac—the notion that opening an oyster shell was a symbol of or preamble to seducing a woman.

In early America, the sturdy shellfish was transported dead or alive by sleigh, wagon and boat—canned or packed in ice, seawater and even sawdust. Such shipments were reaching Chicago as early as the 1830s, despite the arduous journey that involved. With the growth of railroads in the 1850s, however, shipping huge quantities of live oysters throughout the country became inexpensive and increasingly common. Charles Mackay, an English visitor to the United States, remarked in 1857 that "the rich consume oysters and champaigne; the poorer classes consume oysters and lager bier."

It's no surprise, then, that by the 1860s, Chicago was awash in oysters because it was the center of the emerging rail network. In addition, it had strong cultural roots in New England and financial ties to New York, both on the East Coast, where oysters were harvested. Practically every eatery served them. At bars, taverns and dedicated oyster houses, they could be had by the dozen for pennies. Some restaurants used them to entice customers, and taverns frequently gave them away—as long as the customer kept drinking.

The finer restaurants made an art of preparing and presenting oysters. Chefs offered them raw, baked, fried, broiled, steamed, stewed, scalloped, poached, roasted, grilled, boiled, breaded, creamed and more. They threw them in soups, pies, gumbos and omelets. And they served them with innumerable sauces and spices, from alfredo to curry.

The Fourth Annual

COLCHESTER OYSTER FEAST
1930

30TH OCTOBER

THE STEVENS
takes pleasure in again
presenting in America

THE

Colchester
Oyster
Feast

Reproducing that world famous
event which in Old England has
from time immemorial signal-
ized the formal opening of the
Oyster Eating Season.

W. GURNEY BENHAM

Oyster mania lasted decades.
The Stevens (now Hilton)
Hotel held an annual Oyster
Feast recognizing the medieval
England celebration that
heralded the start of oyster
season. *Chicago History Museum.*

Wilson's Oyster House, one of Chicago's earliest fancy restaurants to hang its hat on the oyster craze, opened in 1875 at 21 South Clark Street. Perhaps realizing the marketing potential of Chicago's connection to New England, John Wilson soon renamed his restaurant the Boston Oyster House. Its menu listed no fewer than forty-two different oyster selections and priced a dozen raw oysters at twenty-five cents. The restaurant also served lobster and all manner of seafood.

A cashier at the Boston Oyster House, Charles Rector, must have recognized Chicago's insatiable appetite for oysters when he opened his own place in 1883 a block away at Clark and Monroe Streets. The expensive, high-class restaurant with a large main dining room listed more than twenty cooked oyster preparations on its menu.

Rector ran a seafood restaurant at the 1893 World's Columbian Exposition that received rave reviews, so in 1899, this "oyster maven" opened a restaurant in New York. Rector's on Broadway became celebrated by the well-to-do and gained fame through a scandalous play called *The Girl from Rector's*, which was later turned into a hit Broadway musical.

At some point, Rector's Oyster House in Chicago moved to Adams Street, near State Street. Nearby, the North American Oyster House, seating one thousand, was even larger than Rector's. And the DeJonghe Hotel at 12 East Monroe Street also cashed in on the oyster and seafood trend. This two-block area in the heart of the Loop became a mecca for lovers of oysters and all kinds of seafood.

The amazing Ireland's Oyster House opened in 1900 at 632 North Clark Street. It was not Irish but rather was named after its owner, James Howard Ireland, who decided to serve nothing but seafood to give his restaurant a distinctive character. (Later, he expanded its menu to include meat.) Claiming to be the country's largest exclusive seafood restaurant, Ireland's featured several rooms, including the Lobster Grotto, with an innovative (for its time) live-lobster tank, and the Marine Room, which was a reproduction of the saloon aboard the SS *South American*, a luxury passenger ship. In *Dining in Chicago*, Drury praised Ireland's for serving "every conceivable form of deep-sea delicacy" and recommended the high-quality yet affordable restaurant's popular planked Lake Superior whitefish. During the Depression, patrons packed Ireland's for the $2.75 lobster dinner special.

At some point, Ireland's moved to 500 North LaSalle Street, a handsome red brick building constructed in 1888 as a cable car powerhouse by Charles Tyson Yerkes to drive the miles of cable running underneath city streets that pulled cable cars from 1882 to 1906. For decades, Ireland's was the place to go for oysters and other kinds of seafood, but the restaurant "sank" in the '80s.

The oyster craze lasted well into the '40s, by which time overfishing and pollution had seriously diminished the easy pickings in America's oyster beds. By the '60s, shrimp had eclipsed oysters as Chicago's most popular seafood appetizer. Since the '90s, however, oysters have made a comeback, primarily as a luxury item, but they will never be as ubiquitous as they once were.

CAPE COD ROOM

Rainbo Sea Food Grotto, a new kind of seafood restaurant, opened in 1923 at 117 South Dearborn Street. Decorated with fishnets, portholes and other maritime trappings, and renowned for its waitresses decked out in sailor outfits, Rainbo must have been a fun place to eat. It sparked a wave of similar, over-the-top seafood restaurants around the country.

Following in that wake, the Cape Cod Room at 140 East Walton Street in the plush Drake Hotel got off to a dynamic start, opening on December 6, 1933, the day Prohibition ended. Its extravagant nautical décor celebrated sailing and fishing, New England style. Ben Marshall, a fisherman and the Drake's manager in 1933, went to great lengths to create a fantasy world that resembled a seaside cottage or a cabin on a luxurious yacht. He decorated the restaurant with ship models, copper pots converted into lamps, a weather vane, lobster traps and mounted fish, some of which he had caught himself. Early on, the Cape Cod Room attracted politicians, entertainers and other luminaries. Its large wood bar was famous as a place where celebrities, such as the newly married Marilyn Monroe and Joe DiMaggio, carved their initials.

The Cape Cod Room embodied the idea of a theme restaurant, decorated to the gills with nautical knickknacks and sailing gear. *Author's collection.*

Eventually, the Cape Cod Room outdid all of Chicago's other seafood restaurants in terms of fame and longevity. Specialties of the house included Bookbinder Soup (made with red snapper and served with a cruet of sherry), Lobster Thermidor (with mashed potatoes) and Dover Sole Meuniere (prepared tableside). All these specialties were kept on the menu from opening day forward.

This strong, traditional menu instilled an uncommon loyalty among the dining public. Some customers also liked the cozy booths, comfortable setting and formal atmosphere, with waiters dressed in coat and tie. Others grumbled that the only thing that ever changed at the Cape Cod Room was the prices. This lack of change made the Cape Cod Room eventually feel stiff and staid. The venerable institution, which had become synonymous with the finest, freshest fish, sailed for the last time on New Year's Eve 2016, an event during which tears flowed, along with champagne. The restaurant was so beloved that the decorations and bar, with so many initials carved into it, were saved.

Because of the Cape Cod Room's fame, it's easy to forget that the Drake had other restaurants. The Raleigh Rooms was its coffee shop, and the still-open Coq d'Or boasts of having Chicago liquor license number two.

BERGHOFF

For decades, the thought of fine dining downtown brought to mind three big "Bs": Berghoff, Binyon's and Blackhawk. The Berghoff is still open, but it closed for a short time, so it warrants a mention in this book about lost restaurants. The original Berghoff opened in 1898 as a saloon to sell beer that it brewed in Fort Wayne, Indiana—beer that had become popular at the World's Columbian Exposition. In 1913, the Berghoff moved to its current location at 17 West Adams Street. Things went along swimmingly for almost a century.

When the restaurant announced in 2006 that it would close, Chicagoans let out a collective moan on par with the groan that followed Macy's purchase of Marshall Field's department store in 2005. Loyal Berghoff fans lined up for what they thought would be their last meal of sauerbraten, creamed spinach and apple strudel. The haste with which the famous restaurant was reopened, however, caused critics to speculate that the "closure" was designed, in part, to rid the Berghoff of its relatively expensive union waiters.

Those professional men, decked out in starched aprons, contributed greatly to the restaurant's old-world ambiance. Proper and efficient, they were able to remember orders without writing them down. And they used a European payment system in which they bought food from the restaurant and resold it to customers at slightly higher prices. (This meant that customers actually paid their waiter at the end of their meal.) Today, the restaurant continues much as before, without the classic waiters, but with its own beer and roughly the same menu, albeit less Germanic and a bit lighter.

BINYON'S

Binyon's, tucked away at 327 South Plymouth Court, had dining rooms spread over three floors. Family lore has it that in the '30s, Hal Binyon won the building, then a nondescript German restaurant, in a backgammon game. After World War II broke out, Binyon changed the name to Plymouth Rock but continued to serve a limited German menu. Later, a descendent of Hal's renamed the restaurant Binyon's. Over the years, the restaurant

Known for its turtle soup, Binyon's gave way to the Plymouth Bar & Grill, which basks in its proximity to the Harold Washington Library. *Eric Bronsky.*

became famous for hearty German food, in particular braised ox joints and turtle soup spiked with sherry. Being next door to the Chicago Bar Association, across the street from the prestigious Standard Club and a block from the esteemed Union League Club, Binyon's attracted many attorneys, judges and other members of the city's power elite.

The Binyon family sold the restaurant around 1986. The new owners operated under the same name for a while but closed the restaurant a few years later. In 2005, the Liakopoulos family purchased the building and renamed the restaurant Plymouth Bar & Grill. This Greek family has a long history in the restaurant business, including owning the now defunct Golden Apple (at Lincoln and Wellington Avenues) and the long-standing diner White Palace Grill (still open at Canal Street and Roosevelt Road). They converted Plymouth's top floor into a bar and grill that's open-air in the summer, affording great views of the nearby Harold Washington Library, grotesques and all. The Loop "L" regularly rolls by between the library and restaurant, and occasionally a rider will look over and fondly recall Binyon's turtle soup.

BLACKHAWK

Otto Roth opened the six-hundred-seat Blackhawk in 1920 at 139 North Wabash Avenue, in the shadow of the rumbling "L." It was named after the Eighty-Sixth "Blackhawk" Infantry Division, itself named to honor the Native American warrior who fought against the U.S. Army in the early nineteenth century. The restaurant's huge marquee could be seen from blocks away.

"The introduction of live dance orchestras in 1926 spun the sedate dining room into a major Loop attraction almost overnight," Bronsky and Samors wrote. This was especially true when superstation WGN began broadcasting the music live. The show became so popular that Western Union installed a ticker tape to take listener requests from around the country.

There are no reports of the Blackhawk being closed during Prohibition, but during that period the restaurant sold a lot of ginger ale to mix with the booze that customers brought in their flasks.

Don Roth took over management of the Blackhawk after his father died in 1944. He expanded the entertainment from big band to include comedians, magicians, showgirls and excerpts from Broadway musicals. With the rise

The Blackhawk thrived under the shadow of the Chicago "L." From 1922 to 1952, it provided world-class entertainment that was broadcast on WGN-AM. *University of Illinois at Chicago Library.*

of television, however, Americans could be entertained at home, so the restaurant had to find another way to attract customers. The answer was the food itself. In 1952, Roth removed the stage and declared, "The food's the show." He copied two ideas from Lawry's Prime Rib in California: roving carts of prime rib, carved tableside, and a spinning salad bowl. For the latter, servers repeated verbatim this spiel while working over an aluminum bowl they set spinning on a bed of ice:

> *This is our famous Blackhawk spinning salad bowl consisting of twenty-one ingredients, including a variety of fresh pulled greens. First we spin the bowl and apply the basic dressing. Next we add a bit of special seasoning, and then some chopped egg. We mix the salad a total of six times only, very gently, three now and three times later in order not to bruise the tender greens. Next we add some freshly ground pepper and our special blue cheese dressing. We now mix the salad three more times. And serve—topped with anchovies or shrimp.*

The spinning salad bowl became the Blackhawk's trademark, and for years the "special" salad dressing was sold in grocery stores, but no longer.

Roth followed demographic trends by opening additional Blackhawk restaurants, including one in Wheeling in 1969 and another north of the Chicago River at 110 East Pearson Street in the '70s. The original Blackhawk closed in 1984, after sixty-four years, and the Wheeling restaurant closed in 2009, ending the long, broad history of this restaurant group.

Note: The Blackhawk should not be confused with the Blackhawk Lodge (41 East Superior Street), a restaurant opened in 1991 and now closed. It was known for its rustic charm, knotty-pine paneling, wicker furniture, Audubon prints and fieldstone fireplace. Its menu was thoroughly American, featuring such items as root vegetables, corn, pecans and turkey with mashed potatoes and gravy.

Immediately following World War II, several high-end restaurants opened, taking advantage of postwar prosperity. Yes, after the depravations of the Depression and the long war, Chicagoans were ready to eat out more often. The London House, for one, opened in 1946 at 360 North Michigan Avenue. This sophisticated nightclub and moderately expensive restaurant

Normandy House occupied the corner at Chicago and Michigan Avenues, seen here in 1952. Edgar Miller lived above and helped decorate the restaurant. *Th. Desnoyers photo. Krambles-Peterson Archive.*

became one of the country's premier jazz showcases. Popular, noisy and crowded, it put the accent on steaks, chops and roast beef, as well as music and martinis. It took the unusual step of staying open until 4:00 a.m. The ground-floor London House closed during the '70s, but in 2016, a restaurant of the same name opened on the twenty-first and twenty-second floors of the same building. The music and food do not compare with those of the original London House, but the magnificent views up and down the Chicago River make up for that.

Another fine dining restaurant, Normandy House at Chicago and Michigan Avenues (later 744 North Rush Street), is remembered for artist Edgar Miller, who lived above the restaurant. Chicago's "forgotten Renaissance man" actually helped renovate and decorate the restaurant. A 1942 *Tribune* article about conserving sugar to help the war effort noted that the restaurant displayed a poster by Miller that said, "If your sweet tooth you restrain, Then the Axis strives in vain." As for the food, Normandy House was known for tenderloin steak with Roquefort sauce and eggnog pie, a rich custard pie. The restaurant operated from about 1937 until 1956.

FRITZEL'S

Fritzel's (201 North State Street), one of Chicago's most talked about restaurants, also opened right after the war, in 1947. To contrast with wartime shortages, Fritzel's boasted an extensive menu offering more than one hundred items. It even advertised, "Delicious pastries from a modern post-war bakery." And everything on the menu was available at any time that the restaurant was open. Despite being cheek-to-jowl with the noisy Lake Street "L," Fritzel's quickly became the gathering place and watering hole for powerful politicians and influential businessmen. Its patrons were so well connected that police officers knew not to write tickets for cars parked illegally around the restaurant, one officer told the *Tribune* in 1972. Stories abound of politicians and city officials being bribed or paid off at the restaurant.

Fritzel's attracted not only civic and business leaders but also top celebrities, so many that it was often compared with Hollywood's Brown Derby, a famous restaurant patronized by stage and screen stars. Help in the celebrity department came from the fact that Fritzel's was owned by Joe Jacobson and Mike Fritzel, co-owners of the nearby Chez Paree nightclub, which attracted the country's top entertainers.

Mike Fritzel, a co-owner of Fritzel's, "owned a series of nightclubs with possible mob connections," according to *Chicago: A Food Biography. Author's collection.*

Fritzel's attracted the power elite from 1947 to 1972, when the Loop was vibrant. This crowd gathered to celebrate the opening of a new State Street bridge. *Eric Bronsky.*

A new owner took over in 1968, but his timing was bad. White flight, urban renewal and disinvestment in the city center were causing the Loop to deteriorate. Fritzel's closed in 1972, blaming the 1967 fire at McCormick Place, which cut into Chicago's convention business, and the fact that downtown movie theaters had stopped attracting families with "wholesome" movies.

Plans in 2005 to reopen Fritzel's at the same location came to naught. Instead, the Wit, a fashionable boutique hotel, occupies the corner that many people still associate with the iconic Fritzel's.

FROM SECOND CITY TO DINING DESTINATION

Most of Chicago's fine dining restaurants lacked creativity and focused on traditional meat and potatoes. As a result, Chicago remained in the eyes of many a Second City when it came to restaurants. It was frequently compared unfavorably to the country's culinary capitals: New York, New Orleans and San Francisco. This started to change, however, in the early '60s. One factor was Julia Child, who wrote *Mastering the Art of French Cooking* in 1961 and launched her television show, *The French Chef*, in 1963. This stimulated interest not only in French cooking but also good food and fine dining across the board.

Riding this wave, charismatic chef Louis Szathmary, a Hungarian immigrant, opened The Bakery in 1963 at 2218 North Lincoln Avenue in what was then a restaurant desert. This maverick took the unusual approach, at that time, of a chef owning his restaurant and made a name for himself by breaking many restaurant traditions. For example, he served only one entrée per evening, take it or leave it. He used an eclectic mix of cutlery, plates and furniture. He achieved celebrity status and paved the way for

The Bakery was a bit unorthodox—chef owned, offbeat location, no choice of entrée—but its remarkably delicious dishes attracted sold-out crowds. *Eric Bronsky.*

other pioneering chefs, including Jean Banchet and Michael Foley. As more upscale restaurants appeared on the scene, including Printers Row and Maxim's de Paris, Chicago became a mecca for fine dining, recognized for ingenuity by restaurant critics across the country.

GORDON

Gordon at 512 North Clark Street, with a brash interior and eclectic décor, was a big part of this new energy. Although Gordon developed into one of Chicago's most highly regarded restaurants, it had an inauspicious beginning. Deeply in debt, it opened in 1976 in a seedy part of town, wedged between a currency exchange and an adult bookstore. The first chef quit before the restaurant opened; the second one was last seen soon thereafter chasing a waiter down a nearby alley with a knife.

Recently, the restaurant's founder, Gordon Sinclair, admitted that in the beginning he knew nothing about running a restaurant. "The critics said I must have been passionate about food and wine, but the truth is I never liked to cook, drank jug wine and had to intern at another restaurant to figure out how to run Gordon," Sinclair said. "I was so naïve!"

In the beginning, the restaurant's menu had no appetizers and only one soup, one salad, five entrées and a few desserts. Still, Sinclair knew how to promote. Plus, the food was delicious. He had settled on chef John Terczak, who ended up staying seven years. Terczak introduced signature dishes, such as batter-fried artichoke fritters with béarnaise sauce and flourless chocolate cake, later copied all over town. His menu tended toward nouvelle cuisine, with such dishes as "a solitary soft-shell crab in a pool of banana-beef sauce, served on a plate the size of a hubcap," as *Tribune* food critic Phil Vettel wrote in 1989.

After Terczak left, high chef turnover brought additional publicity and kept the offerings fresh. These chefs created a tremendous variety of dishes, such as beef tournedos with hazelnut-crusted sweetbreads; Chilean sea bass served on a bed of red lentils and topped with a dab of herbed yogurt; monkfish "osso bucco"; and barley risotto with port wine syrup and curry oil. Diners expected to be surprised. As the restaurant thrived, it raised the bar for other Chicago eateries.

For a while, Gordon was Chicago's top revenue-producing restaurant. It's credited with sparking the transformation of the once derelict River North

Above: Gordon opened in a seedy part of town but did so well that it expanded and helped create the trendy River North restaurant district, now known as "Eaterville." *Gordon Sinclair.*

Left: "Whenever I dined at Gordon's, I always felt cooler than I really was," food critic Phil Vettel wrote. This menu cover shows it was classy and sassy. *Gordon Sinclair.*

into an entertainment center, packed with trendy restaurants and nightclubs, so many that it became known as "Eaterville" (in contrast to Streeterville, a few blocks east).

Customers kept coming, not only for the inventive dishes but also for Sinclair's flashiness and exuberance. The dapper host had a talent for making customers feel welcome, having fun and running an edgy place. Naughty artwork hung in the restrooms. And when the restaurant celebrated its birthday in 1988 with a '60s party, a six-foot-tall can of Campbell's tomato soup stood outside while black lights pulsed to loud music inside. Decked out in an ivory Nehru jacket, Sinclair distributed daisies, saying, "Peace. Love."

It was "the dapper, unflappable presence of owner Gordon Sinclair, himself, who kept his restaurant sophisticated and vibrant for 23 years," Vettel wrote.

JIMMY'S PLACE

In 1978, a charming opera-themed restaurant opened in an out-of-the-way, industrial district at 3420 North Elston Avenue. Surrounded by vintage opera posters and stained-glass opera signs, patrons at Jimmy's Place could eat fine food while listening to arias. One dining room featured American opera companies and another international companies. Opera devotee Jimmy Rohr ran this sophisticated place, which was noted for touches of French food and French-Asian fusion.

Due to Rohr's severe allergies, Jimmy's Place was the first Chicago restaurant to institute an outright ban on smoking. After eighteen months, however, Rohr realized that the policy was costing him business, so he rescinded the ban in 1992. But he continued to ban perfumes and scents on both men and women. Jimmy's Place required reservations so potential customers could be informed about this policy.

Restaurant critic James Ward wrote, "The most curious thing about Jimmy's Place is that it should be in business at all." There was the incongruous location, the smoking ban and the fact that it seated only forty-four. Yet Jimmy's Place was a smash hit because it placed the highest importance not on glitz and glamour but rather on the quality of the food.

After seventeen years, Rohr closed his restaurant and turned to consulting or, as he put it, "managed care" for restaurants in poor health and

Despite being out of the way at 3420 North Elston Avenue, Jimmy's Place attracted opera lovers with opera music and posters. *Robert Krueger photo. Chicago Public Library, Northside Neighborhood History Collection.*

"babysitting" for restaurateurs who wanted some time off. As for himself, Rohr couldn't afford to quit or take time off because he had to maintain *Callas*, his thirty-eight-foot sailboat named after Maria Callas, the renowned opera singer.

OTHER FINE PLACES

The posh Nick's Fishmarket (Monroe and Clark Streets) also opened in the late '70s. Its claims to fame were an intimate setting and a large selection of fresh fish. The high-priced restaurant on two levels under what was then First National Plaza was intimidating, which fed its reputation as the ultimate power-elite's gathering place in the heart of the Loop. It was the go-to place downtown for VIP treatment and business entertaining. Extra space between the tables allowed for private conversation, tall booths afforded discretion and diners could enjoy intimacy by dimming the lights independently in their booths.

"Nick's shines on its whole-finned fish presentations, which range from farm-raised catfish to exotic denizens of the Pacific," wrote food critic

Lettuce Entertain You gave "goofy" names to its early restaurants. Lawrence of Oregano's menu featured the song "Follow the Bouncing Meat Ball." *Herb Russel.*

Sherman Kaplan in 2001. Like many other restaurants, it fell victim to the Great Recession, in 2009 under a mountain of unpaid rent. A year later, the restaurant reopened as Nick's Fishmarket Grill and Bar in the Merchandise Mart. Waiters shed their tuxedos, and prices were lowered. This less formal approach worked at the new location for seven years.

Lettuce Entertain You Enterprises initially created irreverent restaurants, such as R.J. Grunts (1971–) and Great Gritzbe's Flying Food Show (1974–83). The former is celebrated for its fun-loving menu and photos of its servers on the walls. The latter, with an entirely gray interior, served sandwiches and salads but featured novel cheese and dessert bars.

Lettuce Entertain You's last in a series of self-proclaimed "goofy named restaurants" was Lawrence of Oregano. After that, the company moved into fine dining, starting in 1976 with a reopening of the revered Pump Room, a restaurant known for "putting its best food forward." It was also famous for celebrity sightings that dated back to when the iconic restaurant opened in 1938. An impressive photo wall of fame attested to its appeal to the rich and famous. But the Pump Room is not really a lost restaurant since Lettuce

Above: VIPs, like Playboy founder Hugh Hefner, singer Nancy Sinatra and newspaper columnist Irv Kupcinet, were regulars at the Pump Room's Booth One. *Lettuce Entertain You Enterprises.*

Opposite: "Booth One," a corner table at the Pump Room, was reserved for celebrities such as film critic Roger Ebert and actor John Belushi. *Lettuce Entertain You Enterprises.*

Entertain You revived it—albeit under the name Booth One, which long ago was a table at the Pump Room reserved for top celebrities.

The company's move into high-end restauranting continued in 1980 with the exceptional, expensive and romantic Ambria in the Belden-Stratford Hotel. The year after Ambria closed in 2007, the company opened L2O, a high-end fish restaurant, in the same space, but that closed in 2014.

Drake's Mayors Row (131 North Dearborn Street, close to city hall) was frequented by the political hoi polloi and festooned with political mementos. Its tagline, "Depicting Chicago's Colorful Eras," could have been a reference to itself because Mayors Row had been a speakeasy during Prohibition. The restaurant was easily spotted from the street due to its distinctive two-story black, white and gold sign.

As the Loop deteriorated in the '70s and early '80s, Mayors Row was giving away incredible happy-hour treats, such as spinach soufflé, finger sandwiches, meatballs, deviled eggs, ribs and potato skins. Nevertheless, Mayors Row was torn down, along with the rest of Block 37 in the '80s. It reopened shortly thereafter at 221 North LaSalle Street, still close to city hall. The décor of the second location was more subdued, but photos of Chicago mayors still decorated the walls. It flourished into the '90s.

The upscale Custom House (500 South Dearborn Street) was open from 2005 to 2012. It had a warm contemporary setting and specialized in seasonally inspired dishes with local ingredients, such as corn, squash, fennel, root vegetables and even Chicago's eponymous stinky onion. This made it an early practitioner of the farm-to-table movement. Custom House occupied a corner (where Meli Café is now) that offered sweeping views of the street through floor-to-ceiling windows. Meanwhile, its kitchen was visible in the other direction through large interior windows.

Music lovers miss Rhapsody (1998–2012), another elegant fine dining restaurant. The lovely 250-seat eatery at 65 East Adams Street in Symphony Center featured a glass-enclosed patio that gave way to a tiny open park. The Italian-inspired Tesori took over the space.

WEST LOOP HEATS UP

During the '80s, many fine dining restaurants left the Loop for the suburbs. During the following decade, new ones frequently located west or south of downtown. Opening in 1991, Vivo (838 West Randolph Street) was a pioneer in the West Loop, an area previously full of warehouses, butchers and food wholesalers. This chic Italian restaurant described its setting as "loftish-industrial" and, at the same time, romantic. It certainly was that for any couple lucky enough to score Table 70, an enchanting secretive little spot in an old elevator shaft above the rest of the seating area. It afforded just the right amount of privacy.

Vivo was cutting edge. "Trendy to the max, hip as they come," the *Tribune* said when it opened. "Vivo turned an oddball location into Chicago's newest destination." But its food was as pioneering as its choice of location.

Cutting-edge Vivo was one of the first high-profile restaurants to open in the budding West Randolph Street restaurant district. *Eric Bronsky.*

Its "embellishments" on Italian cuisine "pushed it into the near twilight zone of contemporary dining," wrote Sherman Kaplan in *Chicago's Best Restaurants.* Vivo lasted twenty-five years.

Marché, another early and remarkably successful restaurant in the nascent Randolph Street dining district, opened in 1993. This big boisterous French American restaurant at 833 West Randolph Street was praised for its festive atmosphere, vibrant décor and creative dishes, such as apple cider–braised rabbit with creamy polenta. *Condé Nast Traveler* recognized Marché as one of the "Hottest Restaurants in the Country." Nevertheless, it closed in 2010, citing a decline in business due to the Great Recession.

Kitty corner from Marché at 820 West Randolph Street was Red Light (1996–2011), which specialized in French-Asian fusion cuisine. Jackie Shen, who oversaw both Red Light's and Marché's kitchens, was among Chicago's first celebrity chefs. She was known as the "Queen of Fusion."

Vivo and Marché helped to blaze a restaurant trail into the Fulton Market and West Loop neighborhoods. As more restaurants followed, Randolph Street became known, once again, as "Restaurant Row." Such was the case in the '20s, only back then the moniker applied to a stretch of Randolph Street downtown in the theater district. In the '90s, however, "Restaurant Row" referred to Randolph Street west of Halsted Street.

Still, opening a restaurant in the trendy West Loop was not a sure thing. The Lunatic, the Lover & the Poet (736 West Randolph Street) opened and closed within 2017. This massive restaurant delivered seven thousand square feet, spread over three floors and a wine cellar. It derived its name from a line in Shakespeare's *A Midsummer Night's Dream,* which explained the pithy literary quotes adorning the wall, as well as the way the check was

Above: In the '90s, a warehouse district along Randolph Street west of the Loop began attracting new eateries—and revived the old moniker "Restaurant Row." *Eric Bronsky.*

Left: Scoozi! (410 West Huron Street) was noted for a big red tomato hanging out front. When something in the restaurant was dropped, everyone would say, "Scoozi!" *Lettuce Entertain You Enterprises.*

Randolph Street Restaurant Row, Where 27,000 People Eat Daily.

The early growth of jobs and entertainment downtown created a huge need for restaurants. This 1909 drawing identified Randolph Street from Michigan Avenue to Fifth Avenue (now Wells Street) as "Restaurant Row." *Author's collection.*

delivered in a hollowed-out book. The restaurant was extremely ambitious but did not succeed, critics said, because it placed more focus on its extensive selection of pricey wines than on its food. Also, it could have fallen victim to what by 2017 was an overabundance of restaurants in the West Loop along Randolph Street.

Like the West Loop, the trendy South Loop was also brimming with restaurants in the early 2000s. Opened in 2002, the pan-Asian Opera at 1301 South Wabash Avenue was noteworthy for being housed in an old film warehouse, thereby allowing for tables in former film storage vaults that had been converted into cozy dining nooks. Despite its large dramatic space, good reviews and strong track record, Opera succumbed in 2010 to the economic downturn that cut so deeply into Chicagoans' disposable incomes.

Today, only a few old, fine dining restaurants remain open downtown. Chicagoans can step back in time at Miller's Pub (founded in 1935) on South Wabash Avenue, Berghoff (1898) on Adams Street, Walnut Room (1907) in Macy's on State Street and Italian Village (1927) on Monroe Street.

CHAPTER 6

Sizzling Steakhouses

A t the top of the list of great but gone Chicago restaurants would have to be one brawny steakhouse after another. Chicago has long been wedded to steak, as much as New Orleans to gumbo, Maine to lobster and Boston to baked beans. The rough-and-tumble, meat-and-potatoes City of Broad Shoulders has long served up big, filling portions of hefty beef, with steaks that hang over the edge of the plate—and large plates, at that. Hard work led to full-sized appetites, so it's always been "prime time" in Chicago. Sure, some diners have sipped soup, swallowed oysters, sampled nouvelle cuisine and savored colorful ethnic dishes. But Chicagoans and visitors to the city have always stampeded back to thick, juicy, well-marbled steaks.

STOCK YARD INN

Perhaps the Chicago Union Stock Yard & Transit Co. accounts for some of this appetite for beef. Before it opened in 1865, pork and local game were the most commonly served meats, from taverns to exclusive hotel restaurants. But the stockyards brought mammoth numbers of animals, primarily cattle, to town for slaughter—400 million in its first thirty-five years alone. Many of the choicest cuts of beef ended up on restaurant grills and ranges.

The Hough House predates the Chicago Union Stock Yard, and its restaurant promoted grain-fed beef. The legendary Stock Yard Inn replaced it in 1912. *Chicago Illustrated*, 1866. *Chicago Public Library, Special Collections.*

Before the stockyards were built, Hough House, a massive hotel with a meat-oriented restaurant, opened in 1854 on South Halsted Street. The six-story edifice catered to businessmen, livestock men and visitors at the small stockyards that were already popping up in this underdeveloped area. "The view from the cupola of this hotel is remarkably fine, commanding a view of the lake, the city and the boundless prairie to the south," according to a contemporaneous account.

After construction of the Union Stock Yard, Hough House was renamed Transit House, and its restaurant became famous for serving exceptional meat. In 1878, John Sherman, superintendent of the stockyards, purchased the winner of the city's first livestock show featuring thoroughbred, fattened animals and served it for Christmas at the Transit House, according to Daniel Block and Howard Rosing in *Chicago: A Food Biography*. This "highlights the importance of the hotel, as well as the Union Stock Yard itself, in popularizing [early on] the consumption of grain-fed fattened beef," they wrote.

In 1896, the *Tribune* noted that the Transit House, "instead of impairing the quality of its accommodations, has made itself better, year by year, and is today at the zenith of its popularity." Alas, Transit House was destroyed by a massive fire in 1910 that burned for twenty-four hours. Two years later, the new Tudor-style Stock Yard Inn at 4178 South Halsted Street replaced the hotel. It included the cowboy-themed Sirloin Room, which for decades remained an extremely popular steakhouse. Customers enjoyed choosing a raw steak from an "ice throne" and branding it with their initials.

In 1934, another fire destroyed a large portion of the stockyards, including the Stock Yard Inn, but the inn and its beefery were quickly rebuilt. The Matador Room, which featured bull-fighting paintings and paraphernalia, was added in 1953, and the inn's restaurants served everyone from cowboys to presidents—and maybe even a few bullfighters.

The restaurants were also popular with tourists, who came by the hundreds of thousands a year. Many of them arrived via the Stock Yards Branch "L," toured the slaughterhouses and capped off their day with a succulent steak at the inn. Plus, the restaurants attracted hog farmers and sheep herders, corporate executives and financiers, animal science professors and deans of agricultural schools. In addition, legislators and politicians indubitably struck many history-making deals at the inn's restaurants while attending the five national conventions held at the adjoining International Amphitheater

The Tudor-style Stock Yard Inn, in a view looking northwest along Halsted Street, with the Stock Yard National Bank in the background. *Chicago History Museum.*

during the stockyards' glory days. In 1954, a country and western radio show aired from the Sirloin Room on WMAQ-AM. It featured music as well as interviews with cattle traders and diners.

Of course, all this was not to last. By the time the Union Stock Yard closed in 1971, the restaurants were dilapidated. The inn succumbed in 1976, following the ghosts of more than a billion animals that had passed through the stockyards' gates.

EARLY STEAK RESTAURANTS

Getting to the Sirloin or Matador Rooms was onerous and time-consuming, at least until an "L" route that directly served the stockyards opened in 1908. Also, the area, with its dust and stench, was not necessarily an inviting place to dine. Therefore, restaurateurs built many steakhouses downtown.

Billy Boyle's Chop House at 5 Calhoun Place was open from 1878 to 1895. When Boyle died in 1921, the *Tribune* described him as "the man who taught Chicago to eat beefsteak." Newspapermen hung out at Boyle's, which inspired journalist Henry Hyde to write an honorific poem, "The Chophouse in the Alley."

> *Those were days we all remember.*
> *Those were nights we all must bless.*
> *At the chophouse in the alley,*
> *When the paper's gone to press.*

From at least 1892 to as late as 1900, Abson's English Chophouse at 22 East Jackson Boulevard served steak of "international repute," according to press reports. Given the brick building's nineteen-by-nineteen-foot footprint, the restaurant was cozy, with a first-floor bar, a precariously winding staircase leading to the second-floor dining room and a kitchen on the top floor. A dumbwaiter connected the three floors.

The date of the building's construction is unknown, but it's thought to be shortly after the Chicago Fire. Over the early years, several restaurants occupied the space, including the Red Path Inn, Robinson's and Pickwick Café. "During Prohibition, when patrons customarily gained admittance with a key, its reputation for good cheer remained untarnished," said the *Daily News*. In the '40s, it became 22 East, a "shadowy, removed restaurant…

In the 1890s, Abson's operated from a tiny building that today houses a coffee shop at the end of a quaint lane at 22 East Jackson Boulevard. *Chicago History Museum.*

one of the quietest little retreats in the loop," said the *Tribune.* "The average loop habitué doesn't know it exits."

This is still true today. The anachronistic building stands at the end of a nine-foot-wide brick alley called Pickwick Lane in a setting that brings to mind Harry Potter's magical Platform 9¾. In 2014, Asado Coffee took over this beguiling wrinkle in time, rescuing the charming alley with a sidewalk café. Hero Coffee now runs the café.

WHERE'S THE BEEF?

Because almost all of the best beef ends up for sale in restaurants rather than grocery stores, diners typically ate out to get the juiciest, tenderest steak. They did so eagerly, and memorable steak places proliferated. George Diamond Steak House, first at 512 South Wabash Avenue and then 630 South Wabash Avenue, is remembered for its large, blazing neon sign and its wedge salad with a special house dressing, as well as for its steaks. It was located in the Dexter Building, a prized building by Louis Sullivan and Dankmar Adler. Opened in the '30s, the restaurant lasted until the '90s.

Across the street stood two more steakhouses: Johnny's Prime Steaks at 501 South Wabash Avenue and The Cart at 601 South Wabash Avenue in the Harrison Hotel. To mention a few more outstanding Chicago steakhouses, there was Carmichael's Chicago Steak House at 1052 West Monroe Street; Al Farber's Steak Room (1957–77) at 2300 Lincoln Park West; Fielos Restaurant at 10352 South Western Avenue; and Alexander's Steak House at 3010 East Seventy-Ninth Street that featured weekly jazz sessions. Such places were legion, and most became legendary.

Black Angus at 7127 North Western Avenue was owned by Chris Carson, who popularized carryout ribs, slow cooked over hickory wood. He launched several Carson's The Place for Ribs in Chicago and the suburbs. He also started the Millionaire's Club (19 South Wabash Avenue and other locations), which was a private club open from 1960 to 1980 that became famous for offering unlimited cocktails with meals.

That Steak Joynt at 1610 North Wells Street was another inviting place "to meat." It opened in 1963 in Old Town, when artists, bohemians and entrepreneurs were transforming the ramshackle neighborhood into a colorful hippy hangout full of offbeat shops and eateries. That Steak Joynt's opulent bordello style with its risqué statuary, crystal chandeliers, plush draperies and red wallpaper and carpeting made the restaurant one of the hottest places in town. The Gay Nineties server girls helped build the restaurant's reputation, too. Diners loved the gaslight setting, complete with antiques, stained and etched glass and even a mustachioed piano player grinding out tunes. They also appreciated the hand-carved black walnut bar and the mirrored buffet behind it that previously had served as a display case for Piper's Bakery, which once operated from the same place (and from which Piper's Alley derived its name). It was popular to dine at That Steak Joynt before or after a show at Second City or other nearby music and comedy clubs.

Left: Fielos' huge blinking sign could be seen from blocks away. This photo was taken on St. Patrick's Day as part of City 2000. *Wes Pope photo. University of Illinois at Chicago Library.*

Below: Black Angus (7127 North Western Avenue) had a loyal following and is fondly remembered for steaks and ribs. *Rogers Park/West Ridge Historical Society.*

The restaurant was supposedly haunted, which led to an investigation by the Ghost Research Society in 1993 that confirmed an "inexplicable" cold spot in the restaurant under two Victorian paintings. The organization also took some photos that included inexplicably blurred and misty images. "I have seen these things myself," restaurant manager Raudel Perez told the *Tribune*.

Meanwhile, the restaurant's name almost got it into some real trouble. Soon after That Steak Joynt opened, the Steak Joint in New York threatened a copyright lawsuit. But it turned out to be a "low-stakes" case. The suit was apparently never filed, and the Windy City restaurant later actually thanked the Big Apple restaurant for the free publicity the case generated. That Steak Joynt lasted until 1996.

Ronny's Steak Palace, established in 1963 at 17 West Randolph Street, was quite unusual. Low prices and fast cafeteria service built up a loyal following. The décor changed over the years, and the unusual design near the end caused the *Tribune* in 1997 to compare the place to the *Twilight Zone*. Glowing orange neon lights flickered through ceiling fans, and the tables had large umbrellas, making the restaurant look like an "indoor picnic on Mars." And for a while, the AM Funk Factory discotheque blasted music on the second floor.

Large murals painted for the filming of the 1991 movie *Curly Sue* depicted what appeared to be the story of meat through the ages, showing cavemen huddled over a slab of meat; Mao Zedong sharing beef chop suey with Richard Nixon; and Ronald Regan and Mikhail Gorbachev hailing each other over steak tartare. At one point, there were several Ronny's in the Loop, and one still operates out of the ground floor of the James R. Thompson Center.

The colorful Barney's Market Club was famous for huge steaks, prime rib and lobster. It opened in 1919 at Polk and State Streets and in the late '30s moved to 741 West Randolph Street in the West Loop, where it was popular with politicians, conventioneers and sports fans attending events at the Chicago Stadium. Barney Kessel, the original owner, allegedly had a problem remembering names, so he greeted everyone with, "Yes sir, senator!" The rest of the staff picked up the shtick, which became part of the restaurant's moniker.

Barney's spacious dining rooms had a clubby, masculine feel with deep-grained wood paneling. One of the rooms was called the Senate Chamber. A long dark wood bar at the entrance was kept well polished, and a pianist often played nearby. And a table in the restaurant's "Holy Corner" was reserved for men of the cloth.

Many restaurants claim to be former speakeasies, but Barney's claim is verifiable because Kessel was sentenced to sixty days in jail for bootlegging during Prohibition. Nevertheless, during his sentence, he frequently appeared in his restaurant to greet customers. No, he didn't have a twin; rather, he had a close relationship with the police. When Kessel admitted to being let out some forty times, "the sheriff hotly denied it, testifying, "'Twasn't more than twenty times,'" according to the *Tribune*.

The jolly, rotund restaurateur also got into trouble with the law during World War II when the Office of Price Administration accused him of selling more meat than his ration points allowed. Kessler pleaded that Barney's

The classy Arnie's in Newberry Plaza at 1030 North State Street was opened by Arnie Morton years before he founded the chain Morton's The Steakhouse. *Chicago History Museum.*

was "essential to the war" because so many servicemen dined there. The confrontation seemed to have increased his popularity.

Perhaps falling victim to his own cholesterol-loaded menu, Kessel died of a heart attack in 1951, but the restaurant continued on in his tradition. By the '80s, however, business had fallen off, and it was almost "Goodbye, Senator." The restaurant did close in 1991 but was reopened under the same name, ironically, by a pair of local politicians, Joe Berrios and Sam Panayotovich. Neither of them would ever become a senator, but they kept the fabled political hangout going until 1996. Barney's is gone, but the Haymarket Pub & Brewery in the same building now serves a craft beer called Barney's Centennial IPA.

ARNIE'S AND ELI'S

Two bygone Chicago steakhouses stand out above all others: Arnie's and Eli's The Place for Steak. In 1973, Arnie Morton partnered with Klaus Fritsch to open Arnie's at 1030 North State Street. It had three large dining rooms: the main Art Deco room; a bright garden room with hanging carousel horses and greenery all around; and a white wicker room designed for women, brunch and lunch parties. The restaurant also had an attractive bar with a big dance floor. The place was dazzling but also comfortable, aimed at attracting return customers.

Authors Bronsky and Samors described this restaurant as "a sophisticated, imaginative place," adding that "the one-million-dollar Art Deco motif was as sumptuous as Arnie's straightforward American cuisine." The *Tribune* said in 1994 that the restaurant arrived on the scene "with mirrors blazing, stained glass twinkling, silver glowing, nude paintings beckoning."

Arnie's was known for its superb Sunday brunch, its music and dancing and as a swanky nightspot but mostly for its value and quality. The charming Morton, acting as maître d', attracted customers as much as the excellent yet unpretentious food. Arnie's lasted until 1993, but his last name lives on through the large national chain of Morton's The Steakhouse that he launched in 1978.

Eli's The Place for Steak opened in 1966 in the lobby of the Carriage House. Today, a playlot across the street honors Eli Schulman, the restaurant's founder. *Marc Schulman.*

From 1966 to 2005, Eli's The Place for Steak at 215 East Chicago Avenue was the ultimate place to enjoy a sizzling steak and to see celebrities, famous athletes and powerful politicians. Key to its success was its gregarious owner, Eli Schulman. "When you ate there, you didn't just get Eli's, you got Eli," his son Marc Schulman explained.

Seating eighty, the restaurant was not as large or boisterous as other steakhouses. The dark walls as well as the leather-upholstered chairs and booths gave the place an elegant ambiance, and with Eli working the room, seating customers, chatting with guests, joining parties at their tables, everyone felt welcome and the place came to life.

In addition to steaks and chops, other specialties included the signature dishes of Liver Eli's, shrimp a la Marc (named after his son) and crispy potato pancakes. As soon as they sat down, customers were served a free plate of vegetable crudités and a basket of matzo and raisin pumpernickel. Dessert was an easy choice: cheesecake that was so good it became known as Chicago Style Cheesecake and launched a national brand.

Naturally, many other restaurants, such as the Blackhawk and London House, also served excellent steak, chops and ribs, but they were better known for other features, such as entertainment, a prime location, a long life or a memorable personality.

Today, for a true taste of a classic Chicago steakhouse where the menu might be predictable but the steak predictably pleasing, visit Gene & Georgetti at 500 North Franklin Street. Established in 1941, it's billed as Chicago's oldest steakhouse.

CHAPTER 7

French Food

O *oh la la.* Ever since the United States was founded, Americans have placed French food (and wine) on a pedestal. Thank Thomas Jefferson for that. Patrick Henry said of him, "Jefferson came home from France so Frenchified that he abjured [shunned] his native victuals."

Unpolished Chicagoans in the city's formative years did not shun American food, but at the same time, they appeared to have been impressed with French food. The World's Columbian Exposition of 1893, where Chicagoans were exposed to so many new peoples and foods, generated more interest in French food. For example, one of the hits of the fair was escargot.

DINING IN CHICAGO RESTAURANT GUIDEBOOK

Drury's 1931 Chicago restaurant guidebook hailed the French cuisine as the "greatest cookery in the world" and listed several French restaurants that would "provide the connoisseur of table delicacies with an excelling opportunity to indulge his inclinations towards refined orgy." Escargots Bourguignonne! Moules mariniere! Poulet belle meuniere! Drury could hardly contain himself. This was not gluttony, one of the Seven Deadly Sins, but rather gourmandize.

One of the best established French restaurants at that time was Julien's, noted for its frog legs and salad dressing, the vinaigrette that's nothing like

Le Petit Gourmet was in the Italian Court on Michigan Avenue, a charming venue that was "photographed, drawn and painted more than any other spot in town," according to *Dining in Chicago. Eric Bronsky.*

what's known as French dressing today. The unpretentious restaurant was on the second floor of an old red brick house at 1009 North Rush Street. Meals were served boardinghouse style at long tables by this family-run affair.

Le Petit Gourmet opened in 1921 at 615 North Michigan Avenue in the Italian Court, an open space surrounded by shops and apartments that attracted artists. In this charming venue, "Italian balconies are all about, and the summer sky is above you," Drury wrote, at least when the weather allowed for dining alfresco at the restaurant's little round tables set up in the courtyard. Inside, the restaurant was quaint, with a fireplace, candles and French porcelains decorating the walls. Apparently, the food was not as appealing as the setting. Nevertheless, the well-liked restaurant lasted until 1968, when the courtyard building was razed to make room for an office tower.

The food was excellent, however, at the nearby L'Aiglon at 22 East Ontario Street, opened in 1926. "Why go to Paris when you have L'Aiglon?" Drury asked. Noted for its Parisian atmosphere, with fresh sole shipped in daily from France, L'Aiglon was "too expensive for Bohemians, but patronized largely by the fashionables of the Gold Coast, sleek well-dressed business men from the Loop, as well as celebrities from the stage and opera," he wrote. The restaurant occupied two old brownstone mansions joined together. Each room was used as a dining room, so the place was "as full of private dining rooms, supper rooms, reception rooms and dancing rooms as a castle on the Rhine," Drury wrote. L'Aiglon stood out due to its quality, an extensive wine list (a rarity in those days) and a smattering of authentic Creole dishes on the menu. It didn't close until 1962.

Drury also praised the French restaurant at 180 East Delaware Place (known by its address), calling it "charming and interesting." He liked the extensive menu, fireplace and big table of tempting hors d'oeuvres, "all delightfully atmospheric and redolent of the Old World." But most of all, he liked Jacques Fumagally, the personable maître d'.

In 1935, Fumagally opened his own place, Jacques French Restaurant, at 900 North Michigan Avenue. The food there was often reviewed as exceptional, especially in its early years. The venue was attractive, with three dining rooms and open dining in an inner courtyard. At a time when sidewalk dining was prohibited in Chicago, Jacques became famous for its outdoor seating. "Maybe faux French, but the flower-bedecked courtyard was incredibly popular with the 'Ladies Who Lunch' long before the phrase was coined," wrote the *Tribune* in a 2010 article titled "Top 40 Chicago Restaurants Ever."

Although Drury was impressed with Jacques, years later other critics found the restaurant lacking. By the time French food and wine consultant Alain Maes dined at Jacques in 1968, he declared the cooking lame, a caricature of the Gallic dining experience. "Yes, the ambiance was gentile but the food was phony," from the iceberg lettuce to the "French" salad dressing, and from the hyper-refrigerated food to the lack of expresso, he wrote in his thorough blog, French Virtual Café. Although Jacques may have been coasting for years, it lasted all the way until 1983, making it one of Chicago's longest-running French eateries.

Jacques (900 North Michigan Avenue) operated from 1935 until 1983, making it one of Chicago's longest-running French restaurants. *Author's collection.*

One of Chicago's more unusual early French restaurants was Maillard's, opened in the 1920s as a branch of the noted New York restaurant of the same name that opened in the 1840s. With four large dining rooms in the basement of 308 South Michigan Avenue, Maillard's seated 1,200, making it one of the largest restaurants in Chicago at the time. After it failed during the Depression, the Fred Harvey corporation took over the space and established there its first restaurant that was not affiliated with a railroad station.

Other French restaurants praised in *Dining in Chicago* include Bon Vivant, Café Francaise, Chez Doré, Ciro's Grill and others, all of which demonstrates that Chicagoans of the '20s and '30s—and presumably every era—appreciated fine French food enough to support several expensive establishments.

THE '40s AND '50s

In 1941, Café de Paris opened in a small corner of the Park Dearborn Hotel at 1260 North Dearborn Parkway. The elegant gourmet restaurant was famous for its roasted duckling a la Belasco, flavored with a Cointreau sauce. Henri Charpentir, a longtime chef there, claimed to have created crepes suzette in 1895 when he worked at the Café de Paris in Monte Carlo. When crepes that he was preparing there for the Prince of Wales caught fire, he named the new dish after the beautiful French woman the prince was dining with. "The Prince and his friends were waiting," Charpentir recounted in his autobiography. "How could I begin all over? I tasted it. It was, I thought, the most delicious medley of sweet flavors I had ever tasted."

John Snowden, an African American, opened Le Provencal in 1951 at 1450 East Fifty-Seventh Street. He was a talented chef who had studied cooking in France for more than six years, and his restaurant was a moderately priced outpost that specialized in regional French cooking. Snowden went on to found one of Chicago's greatest cooking schools and train many of the city's top chefs. Le Provencal offered all the classic dishes: escargots, soufflés, bouillabaisse, French onion soup, etc., all prepared "with a true Gallic touch," according to the *Hyde Park Herald*.

Snowden was "the best chef in the city," according to John Terczak, a former student of his and a top chef himself. At the same time, other chefs found Snowden "aloof, arrogant, dictatorial, demanding, intimidating and impatient." Snowden was such a taskmaster that he drove away his workers. Perhaps that's why Le Provencal lasted only about eight years, despite the backing of some investors linked to the nearby University of Chicago.

Today, Hyde Park is pleased to have La Petite Folie (1504 East Fifty-Fifth Street), an upscale restaurant that serves genuine French fare, even though it's in a strip mall. Although it would not measure up to Snowden's standards, it seems like the go-to place to finalize a business deal or celebrate when a professor gets tenure. Students are more likely to eat across the courtyard at Bonjour Café Bakery, a less formal and less expensive restaurant but a delightful place for salade Nicoise, a cassis mousse tart or other light fare.

Café Bonaparte was opened in 1956 at the Sheraton-Blackstone Hotel (now Blackstone Hotel). It was dedicated to Marie-Antoine Careme, one of Napoleon's private chefs, and featured recipes dedicated to Napoleon. This included Phaisan Josephine (named after Napoleon's first wife) and English sole a la Countess Walewska (named after his mistress). The style of this spacious restaurant was pseudo French, including go-go girls and busboys dressed in Napoleonic garb. It met its Waterloo in the early '70s.

THE '60s

The number of French restaurants in Chicago exploded in the '60s, possibly fueled by the 1963 launch of *The French Chef*, Julia Child's television show. Also, Chicago increasingly viewed itself as a global or "world-class" city, so locals welcomed the alluring, sophisticated Gallic gastronomy.

The *fantastique* Café la Tour enjoyed a prime location at the Chicago Water Tower and boasted of an unobstructed view of the iconic tower through two-story picture windows. It was extremely popular, despite being extremely expensive. A *Tribune* critic wrote in 1985 that the service was excellent: "attentive without being intrusive, helpful without being condescending and professional without being aloof." This elegant restaurant was also considered romantic, "terrific for a special night out." And it was open for breakfast, lunch and dinner since the view was always spectacular, especially from a prized window seat. In 1990, Café la Tour opened an adjoining outside café serving its same menu.

MAXIM'S DE PARIS

The ultimate proof of Chicago's new role as a center of French cuisine occurred the same year Café la Tour opened, 1963, when Maxim's de Paris opened a branch in the Windy City—its first franchise anywhere in the world. At that time, Maxim's was perhaps the world's most famous restaurant and had been sung about in popular music, featured in motion pictures, declared an altar to French cuisine and described as a French national treasure.

Opened in Paris during the 1890s, the original Maxim's catered to wealthy locals and tourists and earned a racy reputation. The new Maxim's de Paris in the Astor Tower Hotel at 1300 North Astor Street was a replica of the original one, true in all details except the ceiling. Its intimate subterranean setting afforded no view outside, but the plush décor compensated for that. Everything was lavish: a grand piano underneath a spiral staircase entrance; red velvet banquettes in intimate booths; fleur-de-lis everywhere; and gold molding that seemed to frame everything. At its peak, Maxim's was considered Chicago's best French restaurant; it was certainly among the most expensive.

And who designed the restaurant and the twenty-eight-story building that housed it? None other than Bertrand Goldberg, designer of Marina City. Meanwhile, his Francophile wife, Nancy, operated the restaurant. Chef Pierre Orsi was brought in from France to take command of the kitchen. And what a cuisine: Soles Albert and Poires Helene; bone marrow and sweetbreads; *les fromages et la tarte tatin*. Maxim's became not only an epicurean delight but a celebrity hangout as well. *Tribune* society pages were full of breathless descriptions of the swanky galas held there.

It was not to last, however. After Maxim's closed in 1982, other restaurants tried to make the unique—but by then a bit rundown—space work, but none of them lasted more than two years. In 2000, Nancy gave the restaurant to the city. Subsequently, it was used for cultural affairs, weddings, cabaret nights and literary events, some of which were hosted by the author and intrepid journalist Rick Kogan. Scenes from *Inglorious Basterds* and *Midnight in Paris* were shot at Maxim's.

In 2013, private interests purchased Maxim's, and the space has apparently been closed, although there has been talk of renovating it. In any event, the restaurant had a lasting impact on Chicago. Many of the city's French restaurants were founded by someone who worked at Maxim's. For instance, Alain Sitbon, the chef/owner of Le Petit Paris, came to Chicago at the age

When Maxim's de Paris decided to franchise, it built a replica—dripping in red and gold—in a Bertrand Goldberg building at 1300 North Astor Street. *John W. Sisson Jr. photo. Chicago Department of Cultural Affairs and Special Events.*

of eighteen to work at Maxim's. George "Kiki" Cuisance, of Kiki's Bistro, moved to the United States to work at Maxim's as a sommelier. And Jean Joho, of Everest, today's ultimate French restaurant, got his start there, too. (All three of these restaurants are still open.)

In 1964, the demanding chef John Snowden, formerly head chef of Le Provencal, tried again with Café la Cloche at 1533 North Wells Street in Old Town. This time, he owned a share of the restaurant in the hope of being able to insist on his high standards. Nevertheless, Café la Cloche closed after a short run. Ironically, it was located two flights above the counterculture-oriented Chances R. What a contrast! One restaurant served burgers, beer and peanuts, while the other served some of the best French food found anywhere this side of the Atlantic Ocean.

CHEZ PAUL

Chez Paul also had a new beginning in 1964. The restaurant opened in 1946 at 180 East Delaware Place but really came into its own after moving eighteen years later to its legendary location in the historic McCormick mansion at 660 North Rush Street. When William Contos took over Chez Paul in 1964, he furnished it with antiques and precious artwork. A devastating fire the following year destroyed most of the building's interior and furnishings,

but Contos restored the mansion's fireplaces, French doors, crystal chandeliers, marble pillars, famed teak staircase and all. He even commissioned artists to repaint many of the lost paintings. For years after that, the elegant and expensive Chez Paul was the place to go. Eating there was a cultural experience as well as a gastronomical indulgence.

At the height of its fame, Chez Paul snagged two scenes in the 1980 film *The Blues Brothers*. In one scene, the Bluesmobile pulls a U-turn into a coveted parking spot right in front of the restaurant. In the other, Jake Blues, played by

Chez Paul operated out of a beautiful 1870s mansion. The elegant restaurant was used to shoot two scenes in *The Blues Brothers*. *Chicago History Museum.*

John Belushi, shatters the classy restaurant's glowing allure by asking a man at the next table over to sell Blues his wife and daughters.

The lovely historic setting could not sustain the restaurant forever. As the years slipped by, the cooking slipped and the setting deteriorated. Contos declined to update the menu. "I don't like nouvelle cuisine," he told the *Sun-Times* in 1987. "It's too dainty, too cute, too pretty. If I'm going to eat a lamb chop, I want it to look like a lamb chop, not with pine nuts and crazy decorations." By the time he died in 1993, his restaurant had dropped from "haughty" to "dull," according to a *Sun-Times* review. Chez Paul closed at the end of 1995.

⸙

Many Chicagoans' favorite French restaurant was the unpretentious L'Escargot (2925 North Halsted Street), which opened in 1968 and specialized in honest "small-town" French Provincial cooking. The cramped place, with pew-like seats and checkered tablecloths, was credited with introducing locals to moderately priced, casual provincial cooking, according to the *Tribune*. Dinner started with a free serving of ratatouille, likely intended to make sure everyone who ate there discovered this tasty treat. But L'Escargot was best known for snails, veal and cassoulet, all equally iconic French dishes that many Chicagoans needed to discover.

"The important thing is not to have just an authentic restaurant, or a money-making one, or a popular one," owner Alan Tutzer was quoted as saying. "The significant professional thing is to have all three." And he did with L'Escargot.

Fire destroyed the restaurant in 1979, and the owners quickly reopened at a fancier address, 701 North Michigan Avenue in the Allerton Hotel. Things must have gone well because in 1983 Tutzer took the unusual step of rebuilding at the original site and then continuing to operate both restaurants. Although the Halsted site was rebuilt with the same casual ambiance as the original restaurant, both sites worked off the same menu. Like brothers, the two restaurants had the same parents and many common traits but their own individual personalities. Both closed in 1993.

KIKI'S RESTAURANTS

Similarly, Le Bordeaux operated two related sites, both the work of George "Kiki" Cuisance, who had arrived in Chicago to help open Maxim's. The one at 3 West Madison Street opened in 1969 and was described as "transplanted France" because it seemed so genuine. Diners remember it in particular for its intimate setting. Le Bordeaux, just a couple of blocks away at 150 North Michigan Avenue, opened in 1988 and had a modern air, well suited for business lunches. Both were subterranean and served the same authentic French fare. Patrons enjoyed terrines, snails, lobster bisque and steak frites, all served with plenty of parsley and butter. "The restaurant's crusty bread served as the perfect sponge to mop up every precious drop of sauce," wrote one reviewer. "This is the place to try sweetbreads," he added for the many Chicagoans indubitably hesitant to try ris de veau or ris d'agneau (thymus or pancreas of calf or lamb, respectively).

When the second Le Bordeaux opened, a critic wrote, "This new addition to the Loop dining scene should quickly become a dependable downtown friend." Unfortunately, downtown dining of all kinds dwindled in the late '80s. But that did not stop Cuisance from his avocation. In 1990, he opened Kiki's Bistro farther north at 900 North Franklin Street. That remains one of Chicago's favorite French restaurants, not just for traditional dishes, such as coq au vin and boeuf bourguignon, but also for innovative dishes, such as grilled rabbit sausage with potato salad, foie gras with lentils and duck terrine with pistachios.

After Kiki's Bistro had been serving Francophiles at the corner of Franklin and Locust Streets for twenty years, the City of Chicago assigned the honorary title of "Rue de Kiki" to the intersection and proclaimed Bastille Day, July 14, 2010, to be George "Kiki" Cuisance Day.

THE '70s AND BEYOND

The formal and upscale Le Perroquet (70 East Walton Street) opened in 1973. Along with Le Français (1973–2007) in Wheeling, it was consistently recognized as one of the best French restaurants, not only in Chicago but the country. Le Perroquet specialized in nouvelle cuisine while Le Français served more classic creations, in particular soufflé. Both were pretentious,

Perroquet more so, with a menu in French, without translations. The prices, however, were easy to read, but probably only for the men since it was common for expensive restaurants to give women a menu without the prices. As expensive as it was, patrons got their money's worth—from les amuse gueules to le plat de résistance to the sorbet (served in the middle of the meal to refresh one's pampered palate) to the Grand Marnier soufflé. Originally, the restaurant offered only one prix-fixe dinner each night, but it expanded on that over the years.

Le Perroquet was known for restraint and elegance but not for an attractive décor or friendliness. Some people were not comfortable with the formality of it all, but customers kept coming, perhaps to impress a business colleague or a date. Whatever the reason, they got an unforgettable experience. Jovan Trboyevic, the chef-owner behind it, also created the immensely successful Jovan and Les Nomades restaurants. Le Perroquet was *le top* but closed in 1991 after a respectable run of eighteen years.

The following year, the highly admired and innovative chef Michael Foley, who had trained in Lyon, the gastronomical capital of France, attempted to resuscitate Le Perroquet. This prompted headlines like "Comeback of the Year." Foley, who was already running the pioneering Printers Row restaurant in the South Loop, told the *Tribune*, "I'm looking to bring Le Perroquet into the nineties. There will be a lot of similarities [to the Le Perroquet of old], but I'm not looking to duplicate."

Foley lightened up the food, relaxed the dress code, introduced menus in both French and English and changed other things in an effort to make the restaurant more accessible and less mystifying. The ambiance went from solemn to cheery and from somber to bright. Regrettably, the new approach didn't work. By the early '90s, Chicago diners were less interested in fancy, expensive French food served in a traditional manner. Casual was in, so Le Perroquet closed for good in 1994. All the years it was open, however, this tasteful place with its haute cuisine played a big role in maintaining Chicago's reputation as a cosmopolitan city.

In 1975, chef Francis Leroux took over the rustic La Gare Saint Lazare (858 West Armitage Avenue). At that time, the area had not gentrified, so this restaurant was a delight in a gastronomic desert, Maes blogged. "I was seduced by the simplicity and refreshing lack of pretension of French comfort food served at very reasonable prices." Others fondly remember the pâtés. Fire destroyed the restaurant in 1987.

By 1979, French cuisine ruled the fine dining scene. That year, five of Chicago's best seven restaurants were French, according to a *Chicago Magazine* reader survey. *Bien sûr*, Le Perroquet was one of them. Ambria at 2300 Lincoln Park West would surely have made the list, too, except that this bit of bliss did not open until the following year. The highly acclaimed Ambria was described as luxurious but not ostentatious, polished but not pompous. "Dining there is like wrapping yourself in a warmly inviting culinary quilt," wrote *Sun-Times* food critic Pat Bruno.

Founding chef Gabino Sotelino served up moderately expensive French dishes with creative touches. Unusually inventive. Often surprising. Always delicious, beautifully garnished and well presented. After twenty-seven years, Ambria was still doing well and making money, but Sotelino decided to pull the plug anyway, saying, "You need to leave when you're on top."

Across the lobby of the building, one could enjoy a different approach to French food at the relaxed Un Grand Café, where the ambiance was that of a friendly bustling bistro. The food was less inventive, less *travaillé*, but all the while delightful and delicious. In 1998, the owner, Lettuce Entertain You, relaunched the restaurant as Mon Ami Gabi (for chef Gabino Sotelino). It opened up the space and lightened up the menu but changed little else. Mon Ami Gabi is still going strong.

FROM BISTRO 110 TO MARCHÉ

Another great bistro opened in 1987 at 110 East Pearson Street. Bistro 110 was gorgeous, with lots of light and an inviting allure.

"Bistro" and "brasserie" are often used interchangeably but have different meanings. The former is a relaxed neighborhood eatery that serves unassuming food at reasonable prices. It places the emphasis on good food in a modest setting. A brasserie, on the other hand, tends to be larger, louder and more open. It sells simpler food and places the emphasis on drinks. After all, *brasserie* in French also means "brewery."

The food at Bistro 110, much of it prepared in wood-burning ovens, was better than bistro, despite the name of this refined restaurant. Some seating faced the street, and the covered sidewalk patio out front offered comfortable seating, even in the winter.

Tables on a covered sidewalk patio in front of Bistro 110 gave this shoppers' haven a Parisian feeling. They were enclosed for use in the winter. *Lawrence Levy.*

Bistro 110 maintained quality by sending chefs to France every year to learn new recipes. It also invited French chefs to Chicago to take stints in its kitchen. A buzz prevailed that the ample original art adorning the walls had been traded for food by struggling artists, but this was a myth. Bistro 110 went out on a high note in 2011, and its many fans still talk about its pleasant ambiance and exquisite dishes.

Overlapping with Bistro 110 was Cyrano's Bistro & Wine Bar, open from 2006 until 2015 at 546 North Wells Street. Owned and run by chef Didier Durand, this restaurant was less flashy and more modest than other places, but the meals were often better. This was the place to go for rabbit or ratatouille, cassoulet or bouillabaisse and other French favorites. The prix fixe was always a great deal. Over the years, Durand revamped the restaurant, changing the name and décor to reflect a more casual, rustic approach. He moved the operation to 233 East Lower Wacker Drive in 2015 and renamed it Cyrano's Café on the Riverwalk, where for several years it served a delightful, high-quality alternative to some of the other vendors along the river.

Brasserie Jo opened in 1995 at 59 West Hubbard Street. The big, bright, busy restaurant served food with an Alsatian accent, characterized by choucroute and charcuterie, but also snails, fish, pommes frites and onion tart, all typically washed down with beer or light white wine. Especially nice were personal touches. It was dog friendly, just like most restaurants in France. Warm crusty mini baguettes welcomed you as you sat down and could be taken home, as well. The people-watching in this usually crowded cosmopolitan restaurant was as good as the eclectic menu.

As with Gordon, Brasserie Jo opened next door to an adult bookstore. Its success furthered River North's transformation into a restaurant and entertainment hub, something that had begun in 1976 with Gordon. As with many Lettuce Entertain You restaurants, Brasserie Jo was shuttered too early, remaining open only fifteen years, despite being wildly popular. It was replaced by Paris Club, and the location currently houses Il Porcellino.

<hr/>

When Marché opened in the West Loop, it was said to combine the brasserie with the bistro. This loud, vibrant restaurant was quite different than anything Chicago had seen before and quickly became the place to be seen. The layout of the two-level restaurant was whimsical, colorful, even carnival like, with painted columns, heavy drapes and a high ceiling. An oversized bar jutted out from the open kitchen, making it easy to sit and watch the energetic cooking "performance" inside the kitchen. The food was as innovative as the décor: sweetbreads, monkfish, quail with chanterelles, chocolate Armagnac mousse and so on.

It's impossible to cover all the French restaurants here, but they have all helped to make Chicago a gastronomic capital of the world. Here's a nod and a big merci to Bistrot Zinc, Savarin, Bistrot Margot, Café Matou and Rudi's Wine Bar. Rudi's was a warm, casual but sophisticated bistro at 2424 North Ashland Avenue where the authentic French food, extensive wine list, smooth music and cool atmosphere took you right to Paris just by walking through the door.

PHONY FRENCH

One last category of French restaurants that have come and gone over the years would be phony French: either French in name only or stereotypically French rather than genuinely Gallic. They were *les faux amis*. Chez Paree

(1932–60), for example, was a fancy nightclub/restaurant where the menu listed steaks and ribs, not escargot and Roquefort. In any case, Chez Paree patrons were typically more interested in entertainment and celebrity sightings than in food.

Chez Paree opened in 1932 on the third floor of a warehouse at 610 Fairbanks Court and closed in 1960. On opening night, superstar Sophie Tucker christened the place by breaking a bottle of champagne on its front door, proclaiming, "Revelry is in order." Chez Paree remained Chicago's premier nightclub for three decades, and Tucker made more than a dozen return performances. Joining her were Pearl Bailey, Nat King Cole, Ella Fitzgerald, Jackie Gleason, Bob Hope, Mickey Rooney and many other big names. No wonder the place was called "Stairway to the Stars." It also featured chorus girls called the Adorables who danced in "scanty, flashing finery."

The restaurant had its ups and downs but kept coming back, once under the moniker "Chez It Again." Toward the end of its life, when the party was just about over, it was still known as one of the few places (other than a charity ball) where one could dress to the nines and fit in.

Meanwhile, The Little Corporal at 1 East Wacker Drive was a snack place with hardly any French menu items. Instead, it had kitschy Napoleonic

Chez Paree was on the third floor of this warehouse (seen here in 1956). Despite the setting, it was Chicago's premier nightclub for three decades. *Chicago History Museum.*

AMERICA'S SMARTEST THEATRE RESTAURANT

CHEZ PAREE, 610 FAIRBANKS COURT, CHICAGO, ILL.

Above: Chez Paree was swanky and for a while featured chorus girls called the "Adorables" who danced in "scanty, flashing finery." *Author's collection.*

Left: The Little Corporal was a twenty-four-hour restaurant decorated as an opulent but misguided homage to Napoleon. *Eric Bronsky.*

decorations galore. Paintings of Napoleon's exploits decorated the walls. A six-foot-wide Napoleonic bicorn hat dangled from the ceiling in one of the dining rooms. The exterior of the ground-floor restaurant was decorated with Napoleonic insignias. And the menu, decorated with medals, was shaped like Napoleon's uniform. Nonetheless, the restaurant was extremely successful from when it opened in 1964 until it closed in the '80s, probably because it was fast and efficient—and open twenty-four hours a day, with an adjoining 4:00 a.m. cocktail lounge.

Finally, there were several "French" restaurants in the '50s and '60s that were really more continental than authentically French, despite their names. Many of these were run by a partnership between Ray Castro and Edison Dick, which at its peak managed or owned sixteen restaurants, the majority of which had French names. Despite the commercial success of this enterprise, "many serious critics and cognoscenti…admit that the Castro Group restaurants were more pretending to be French than authentically French," Maes wrote in his blog. This would have included Mon Petit (1255 North State Street), Biggs (1150 North Dearborn Street), Maison Lafite (1255 North State Street) and Le Mignon (712 North Rush Street). At least these restaurants introduced many Chicagoans to the idea of French food.

French cooking began to lose its supremacy in the '80s when customers seemed to prefer a simpler, easier dining experience, when they began to favor grazing and grilling over long, drawn-out masterpiece meals. Along the way, Italian and more recently Asian cuisines began to command center stage. Meanwhile, comfort foods and meat and potatoes have made a comeback, giving steakhouses a boost. Also, ethnic restaurants continue to appeal, and fusion of different ethnic cuisines and cooking styles has joined the cuisine cacophony.

CHAPTER 8

Ethnic Eateries

hicago has a huge variety of ethnic restaurants because it's been home to continuous waves of immigrants. These settlers and their descendants expressed their ethnic heritage through stores, churches, clubs, festivals, newspapers and neighborhood associations, but restaurants represented one of the strongest manifestations of their identity. The immigrants and their restaurants turned Chicago into the country's foremost cosmopolitan culinary capital.

Most ethnic restaurants were aimed at feeding folks from their country. The '60s and '70s, however, saw a marked interest in ethnic food across the board. This entailed a learning curve as Chicagoans from one background ventured to sample the food of another. Evidence of this can be found in a 1963 *Tribune* restaurant review that considered it necessary to describe "guacamole" and "nachos" ("an unusual dip made of avocados, onions, peppers and spices" and "an interesting appetizer that looks something like a miniature pizza," respectively). Other reviews likewise described baklava, borscht and brie for adventurous diners. Meanwhile, author and restaurant historian Eric Bronsky noted that the 1971–72 Yellow Pages (remember that?) listed Parthenon Gyros, a North Side branch of the famed Greektown restaurant, under "Gyroscopes."

In the '60s, Chicagoans "discovered" ethnic foods. They faced a learning curve, as demonstrated by this listing for gyros under "Gyroscopes." *Eric Bronsky.*

Despite the challenges, Chicagoans learned to appreciate different ethnic foods—as well as the people and cultures they represented. Food is a powerful and enjoyable force for bringing people together.

GERMAN

For about fifty years, starting in the 1840s, Germans made up the largest number of immigrants to Chicago. In the late 1800s, German was taught in public schools and spoken in stores and restaurants all over town. Municipal signs were routinely printed in German, as well as English. And by 1900, one-fourth of Chicagoans were born in Germany or had a parent who was born there.

German immigrants tended to be middle-class, skilled workers and relatively affluent. They could afford to eat out and took great pride in building and patronizing their own eating and drinking establishments. They brought with them old-world customs, preferences…and recipes. The Teutonic cuisine emphasizes meat and potatoes, and German restaurants have a convivial ambiance, with frothy beer and spirited music. This warm fellowship is called *gemütlichkeit*.

Red Star Inn

Chicago's German immigrants established more than 60 breweries and 140 restaurants or places serving German-style food. Foremost among them was the Red Star Inn (1528 North Clark Street), which anchored the early German American community that was centered on Clark Street and North Avenue (aka German Broadway). It opened in 1899 under its original name, Zum Roten Stern ("to the red star"). Its beautiful gabled, spiraled-brick building had a big red star outside over the entrance. Modeled on a traditional Bavarian tavern, the Red Star Inn's dark, roughly hewn interior featured leaded stained-glass windows; Tiffany light fixtures; wrought-iron chandeliers; beer barrels; elk antlers; and heavy wood tables. Waiters wore tuxedos, not lederhosen. Over the years, the cuisine remained solidly German, serving wurst, apple pancakes and hoppel-poppel, a signature dish of meat, potatoes, onions and eggs that was prepared the traditional way: with leftovers.

Urban renewal razed the Red Star Inn (*left*) in 1970 to make room for Carl Sandburg Village, but the Germania Club (*right*) was spared. *Chicago History Museum.*

Carl Gallauer, the restaurant's founder, was Chicago's acknowledged king of German eateries. A story from his era illustrates the restaurant's stature. When Prince Henry, a younger brother of Kaiser Wilhelm, visited Chicago in 1902, a huge reception was held in his honor at the stately Germania Club. At one point during the festivities, however, someone noticed that the prince was missing. He had slipped across the street to the Red Star Inn for lunch, "such was the fame of the popular restaurant," the *Tribune* reported. (On the same visit, Henry also visited the notorious high-class Everleigh Club, where he allegedly instigated the custom of drinking champagne out of a lady's shoe.)

After Carl died in 1936, his son William took over the restaurant and maintained its class and authenticity. Over the years, he refused to modernize and banned jukeboxes, televisions and even air conditioning. Live music and dancing were also verboten. Still, William kept the restaurant going for several decades—until the Chicago Department of Urban Renewal determined that the handsome three-story building had "no intrinsic merit"! William fought back, insisting, "We don't intend to be pushed around," but his efforts were doomed. The Red Star Inn was forced to close in 1970, and the wrecking ball destroyed its storied building. In the end, the confiscated property only served to expand the entrance to the new Carl Sandburg Village.

The old-fashioned restaurant was so esteemed, however, that it was afforded a second chance. The Riggio family of restaurateurs acquired rights to the name and recipes; purchased wood carvings, wine barrels and other artifacts from the original restaurant; and opened a new Red Star Inn at Keeler Avenue and Irving Park Road. John Riggio even spent three months in Germany perfecting the recipes. The new place opened in 1972 and lasted ten years.

Near the original Red Star Inn and part of that same community, the Golden Ox at 1578 North Clybourn Avenue was another local landmark. It was founded in 1921 and lasted through years of neighborhood decline and urban renewal. Despite its hearty food and striking décor—which included cuckoo clocks, colorful steins, Hummel figurines and murals of scenes from the *Ring of the Nibelungen*, as well as leather chairs and gold tablecloths—the Golden Ox served its last sauerbraten in the '90s.

Old Heidelberg

Eitel's Old Heidelberg restaurant grew out of the Century of Progress, where in 1933 it operated a large restaurant in the German Village. Once Prohibition was repealed in 1933, the restaurant added an extensive beer garden for the fair's second year. The place was so popular that in 1934, the owners opened a restaurant downtown at 14 West Randolph Street in the former Randolph (movie) Theater. The Old Heidelberg added a quirky German-looking façade that included a clock with figures that moved every quarter hour, as a song played. For years, the Old Heidelberg dished out spätzle, wiener schnitzel and other filling favorites to enthusiastic eaters. It also boasted lively music, such as organ playing in the main dining room and singers in the rathskeller.

In 1958, new owner Gus Allgauer took over and renovated the restaurant, but his Old Heidelberg continued the original style of food and entertainment. In 1963, the restaurant gave way to Ronny's Steak Palace, which was followed by the Noble Fool Theater around 2000. Today, Argo Tea makes great use of the picturesque façade, which is the only remnant of the Old Heidelberg.

Over the years, Gambrinus, a medieval king and the mythical inventor of beer, welcomed visitors to the building. The wood figure, designed by local

Left: A 1956 menu cover from the Old Heidelberg indicates how lively and full of music this downtown restaurant was. *Chicago History Museum.*

Below: This fanciful façade was designed by none other than Holabird and Roche in 1923. Once it housed the Old Heidelberg, now Argo Tea. *Eric Bronsky.*

Gambrinus, the mythical inventor of beer designed by Edgar Miller, makes occasional appearances from his perch above the entrance to the former Old Heidelberg. *Wendy Bright.*

artist Edgar Miller, emerged every half hour from a perch above the front door. Gambrinus still emerges like a cuckoo clock every evening at 6:00 p.m., accompanied by chiming music.

"Gambrinus is actually a tad dull," said Wendy Bright, of the WendyCityChicago blog and tours. "The music begins playing, usually some schmaltzy show tune and the doors open. He S L O W L Y slides out and stands there briefly, with his beer belly extended for a minute while the music keeps playing. Still, this is quite an unexpected treat for anyone who happens to walk by."

Lakeview

As Chicago's German Americans moved northwest, a vibrant Teutonic community developed in Lakeview, complete with several old-world restaurants, bierstubes, delis and bakeries. One of the most prominent,

Math Igler's Casino and Restaurant at 1627 West Melrose Avenue, opened in 1923. This Bavarian outpost was known as the "Home of the Singing Waiters"—yes, waiters who sang and singers who waited (waited on tables, that is). Accomplished in both tasks and decked out in lederhosen, these men would perform onstage a couple of times a night, accompanied by an organ, and often engage their patrons in song. Occasionally, they would burst out in spontaneous song individually.

Many of these waiters had performed in opera and famous choral groups. They took requests and sang in multiple languages, including Swedish, Spanish, French, Italian and Gaelic. In addition to German favorites, these "dish jockeys" sang everything from pop to opera—from "Ach, du Lieber Augustin" to "You Ain't Nothin' but a Schweinhund!"

Why the iconic place was called a casino is not clear, as there are no reports of gambling on the premises. But Math Igler's flourished until the mid-'80s.

Math Igler's, "Home of the Singing Waiters," was popular with local German Americans and busloads of tourists. *Robert Krueger photo. Chicago Public Library, Northside Neighborhood History Collection.*

Zum Deutschen Eck ("to the German corner") also had a great run in Lakeview, starting in 1956. Although located at 2924 North Southport Street, this remarkable bastion of Bavarian bravado resembled an inn in Old Munich. It served traditional German fare at modest prices. The lounge, with a bar handcrafted from solid oak, was often a buoyant, boisterous place. Rustic chandeliers hung from wood-beamed ceilings. Steins, painted plates and vases full of flowers decorated the place, along with stained-glass windows and murals depicting pastoral scenes of the old country.

Even more memorable than its décor was Zum Deutschen Eck's *gemütlichkeit*, that comfortable ambiance. Bartenders were jovial, waiters were friendly and the waitresses would flit around in traditional dirndl dresses, flirting with patrons. On weekends, a five-piece oom-pah-pah band played and occasionally led a vigorous singalong.

Zum Deutschen Eck's three banquet rooms and two dining rooms entertained innumerable busloads of tourists. But it was also a neighborhood restaurant serving local Germans genuine food, judging from the amount of German spoken there and the care that the owners, the Wirth family, put into creating an unaffected old-world atmosphere. Good food, good cheer, good drink. *Prost*!

Sometimes the joviality went too far and even had a dark edge. Tucked in behind the façade of the building were speakers that frequently flooded the street with marching tunes and Bavarian drinking songs. And according

Zum Deutschen Eck was an anchor of the North Side German community. All that's left today are a plaque and honorary street sign. *Chicago History Museum.*

to a former employee, it also hosted annual birthday parties for one Adolf Hitler.

Still, along with other nearby German institutions, including Dinkel's Bakery, Paulina Market (a butcher shop) and two delis (Meyer and Kuhn's), Zum Deutschen Eck celebrated Lakeview's German community. Despite a dwindling number of German Americans and renovations in the mid-'80s to lighten the heavy food and tone down the overbearing décor, the restaurant closed in 2000 to make room for, regrettably, a parking lot. All that's left—besides the vibrant memories—are a plaque and an honorary street sign on George Street that says "Zum Deutschen Eck Strasse."

Beer Gardens

Beer was at the center of German socializing and dining. Taverns may not have offered top-quality food, but they were ubiquitous and well patronized, often by the whole family on Sunday. Also popular for eating and drinking on Sunday were the large outdoor beer gardens that re-created a bit of Germany in Chicago. Although not restaurants in the traditional sense, these gardens served food. The Old Vienna opened in 1894 at Sixtieth Street and Cottage Grove Avenue as a direct outgrowth of the World's Columbian Exposition. That garden expanded into Sans Souci, an amusement park named after Frederick the Great's palace. It provided al fresco dining and facilities for dancing and musical performances. Later, a tea garden and roller coasters were added.

In 1914, Sans Souci reopened as Midway Gardens, a large indoor-outdoor restaurant and concert venue designed by none other than Frank Lloyd Wright. This upscale complex featured fine dining, drinking, dancing and top entertainment. A couple could spend all day there, regardless of the weather, taking in everything from afternoon tea to dinner and dancing to a show. Alas, Midway Gardens was done in by Prohibition and changing tastes. After two different owners failed to make it work, the stunningly attractive pleasure ground was bulldozed in 1929.

Many other outdoor beer gardens served food to immigrant families and their friends. Some accommodated more than four thousand patrons at a time, often filling an entire city block. Opened in 1894, the Bismarck Garden restaurant and concert hall at Grace and Halsted Streets featured fountains, a full-size windmill and the largest outdoor wood dance floor in Chicago. It was renamed Marigold Garden in 1917 and closed in 1923 at a

Although designed by Frank Lloyd Wright, the stunningly attractive Midway Gardens in Hyde Park was bulldozed in 1929. *Chicago History Museum.*

time when Prohibition and anti-German sentiments conspired against such establishments.

Another German outdoor eating and drinking venue that closed during Prohibition was the outdoor Moulin Rouge Gardens at 4812 North Clark Street. In 1921, Fred Mann built a nightclub/restaurant there called Mann's Million Dollar Rainbo Room. Years later, the site became famous when an arena was built there that later morphed into the popular Rainbo Roller Rink. (The lack of a "w" in the name remains a mystery.)

GREEK

Greektown once housed more than thirty thousand Greek Americans and scores of restaurants, nightclubs and cafés. Its restaurants, now huddled around a stretch of South Halsted Street between Van Buren and Monroe Streets, tend to be energetic and celebratory. They are characterized by attractive décors, a steady buzz of conversation and a warm hustle and bustle. Competent waiters serve plates of food professionally and refill glasses of wine quickly. And crowning the spirited experience is "Opa," the practice of serving saganaki, a fried-cheese appetizer, flamed to a jubilant chorus of "Opa."

Saganaki is a Greek dish, but the practice of serving it flaming—with sass and style—is not. The festive ritual was invented in Chicago, and this popular practice—some say gimmick—has been copied by Greek restaurants all over the world, even in Greece. Clearly, everyone welcomes Greeks bearing dishes of flaming cheese.

The bygone Parthenon at 314 South Halsted Street is widely credited with inventing in 1968 the flaming saganaki and "Opa" custom. It also claims to have brought the gyro to Chicago. Being named after a Greek treasure on top of the Acropolis of Athens, the Parthenon was appropriately tops for food quality, comprehensive menu and affable service. Also, for years Parthenon was the oldest restaurant in Greektown, having been established in 1968. But such bragging rights were not enough to save the venerable restaurant. In 2016, after feeding and entertaining patrons for forty-eight years, this Greektown fixture closed amid a swirl of problems, including failed health inspections, lawsuits and reported allegations from state and federal authorities of back taxes. Other top Greektown restaurants that have closed include Hellas, Pegasus and Grecian Gardens.

Another lost Greek restaurant, Dianna's Opaa (212 South Halsted Street), starred the outgoing owner and maître d' Petros Kogeones (who also claimed to have invented flaming saganaki). This beloved institution opened in 1972 and soon became the most popular restaurant in Greektown, mostly due to Kogeones's hospitable spirit and theatrics. Meanwhile, urban renewal, highway construction and the expansion of the University of Illinois at Chicago cut into Greektown. Dianna's Opaa closed in 1993 and reopened as Petros Dianna's at 1633 North Halsted Street, another apparent sign of Greektown's demise.

A new but short-lived Greektown developed on the North Side starting in the '70s near the intersection of Lincoln and Western Avenues, but none of these restaurants lasted long. There were Grecian Psistaria and two Family House eateries within half a block of each other. And Athens, a nightclub at 4726 North Western Avenue, did a brisk business in the '70s thanks to the good food and live music every night of the week. The belly dancers didn't hurt, either. "Belly dancing is a Turkish thing, really," owner Simeon Frangos told the *Tribune* in 1974. "But if that's what the Americans want, we'll give it to them."

Greektown's Parthenon claimed to have started the practice of serving saganaki flambé to a loud chorus of "Opa!" *Eric Bronsky.*

Elsewhere around town, Papagus Grecian Taverna (620 North State Street) served food that was more creative than authentic. It was more expensive than the Greektown eateries and seemed like a suburban version of an urban ethnic restaurant. Indeed, the River North location closed and another one opened in Oak Brook.

The remarkable Deni's Den (2941 North Clark Street) thrived for some eighteen years, doing a wonderful job promoting Hellenic culture and cuisine. White walls and hanging plants gave Deni's Den the feel of a Grecian garden. Billed as a sophisticated supper club, its forte was live music. Three-tiered seating oriented toward the stage and dance floor was designed to let diners appreciate the show, which embraced ethnic music, poetry and theater discussions.

The energetic music at Deni's Den was not meant to play in the background; rather, it demanded your attention. While it was playing, patrons were as likely to see elderly Greeks swaying to a slow ballad as to see college students dancing blindly to the lively music of a bouzouki. On the weekends, the party continued until four o'clock in the morning. One could always find a show at Deni's Den after the show.

Meanwhile, the traditional Greektown on South Halsted Street kept dishing out taramosalata, dolmades, braised lamb, moussaka, spanakopita and, obviously, saganaki. Today, Greektown is a magnet for hungry, fun-loving locals and tourists alike. Greek Islands (200 South Halsted Street) opened in 1971 and claims to be the most popular Greek restaurant in the country, with more than half a million customers a year. Athena (212 South Halsted Street) opened in 1997 and features a lovely outdoor patio with an impressive fountain. Greektown's future has recently become more secure thanks to the construction there of the National Hellenic Museum, as well as the unlikely revival of the West Loop. Yes, count on Greektown restaurants to continue "carrying the torch," with "Opa" leading the way.

An addendum: The influence of Greek immigrants on Chicago's restaurant scene spread far beyond restaurants that served Greek specialties. These immigrants worked in and owned all kinds of restaurants around the city. In the '50s, Greek Americans owned an astonishing 85 percent of restaurants in the Loop. Although not as dominant today, they continue to have a significant presence in the industry.

POLISH

Polish immigrants also contributed mightily to Chicago's culinary melting pot. Among the largest immigrant groups, the Poles introduced Chicagoans to a host of traditional dishes such as pierogi, cabbage rolls and kielbasa.

One of Chicago's most fondly remembered Polish restaurants is the Busy Bee at 1546 North Damen Avenue, next to the quaint, original Damen "L" station. It specialized in basic Polish food, or "peasant-style food," as one reviewer put it. There was always a din of clattering plates and loud discussions in the small restaurant, which had a long counter lined with stools and tables against the wall. Everyone from the dregs to school kids ate at this typically crowded neighborhood gathering place. Groucho Marx reportedly was a regular, and it's likely that Nelson Algren dropped in, too, despite the harsh treatment he often gave Poles in his novels set in this community.

Hillary Clinton also ate at the Busy Bee. In 1992, during a campaign stop there for her husband's presidential race, she made her famous comment that being in politics was better than having "stayed home and baked cookies."

One reviewer called this restaurant "the safest place to eat in Chicago because there's always cops eating there." Another recounted a time when an employee called the police for a minor incident, and within minutes, several squad cars arrived on the scene, apparently to serve and protect a favorite restaurant.

Besides safe, the Busy Bee was affordable, especially since no one left the place hungry. "I liked the Busy Bee because it was a comfortable place," said Mary Wisniewski, the *Tribune*'s transportation writer. "I always ordered the pierogi plate because it fit into my City News budget."

Sophie Madej ran the restaurant from the time she bought it in 1965 until it closed in 1998. Everyone described her as lively, nice and welcoming. Madej wasn't the only person crying when the restaurant closed, as the neighborhood was changing from Polish to hipster. "I cooked like I did at home…out of my head from what my mother used to do," she reminisced. "We were open 365 days a year. The Busy Bee was a way of life."

The most elegant Polish restaurant with the best food and service was Turewicz, according to many critics. "Top cuisine this side of Warsaw," said the *Tribune*. A moderately priced family place, Turewicz opened in 1970 at 1643 North Milwaukee Avenue, in the heart of the old Polish American neighborhood. The attractive restaurant was in an unimposing former warehouse and featured red-and-white tablecloths, the Polish national colors. It offered solid food, including old-world recipes, such as tripe, duck's blood soup and bean borscht, served with mead or flavored vodka.

When enough Poles gathered at Turewicz, the musician owners would break out an accordion and a violin, play some gypsy music or pass out song sheets for a singalong. The place was also known to put on fencing demonstrations, originated as a tie-in to the swashbuckling Polish movie *Pan Wolodyjowski* that was playing nearby at the Milford Theater. It's not known how long this restaurant lasted, but no record of it beyond the '70s could be found.

Several excellent restaurants still serve up authentic Polish food, including Staropolska (3030 North Milwaukee Avenue), Podhalanka (1549 West Division Street) and Red Apple Buffet (3121 North Milwaukee Avenue).

ITALIAN

Chicago never received as many Italian immigrants as Polish, German or Irish ones, but you'd never know it from the great number of Italian restaurants that have graced the city. In 1875, 22 of the 176 restaurants in the city directory were Italian, and that number grew continuously and dramatically in the following century and a half.

One of the longest-lived, Madame Galli (18 East Illinois Street), opened at the time of the World's Columbian Exposition. It's credited with introducing Chicagoans to spaghetti, which was greatly appreciated by the famous Italian operatic tenor Enrico Caruso, who ate there regularly. Legend has it that Carmelinda Galli once told him, "Signor, I'd give the world to sing like you," to which Caruso replied, "Madame, I'd give the world if I could cook spaghetti like you."

In fact, Galli began with a boardinghouse, but her spaghetti sauce was so good that it spawned the restaurant. She kept her recipe secret, even refusing to sell it to the keenly interested H.J. Heinz Co. for what restaurant critic John Drury described as a "not unflattering figure."

Madame Galli opened in 1893, back when spaghetti was spaghetti, not "pasta." Heinz Co. tried to buy the restaurant's recipe for tomato sauce, to no avail. *George Krambles photo. Krambles-Peterson Archive.*

Like some restaurants at that time, Madame Galli had no menu. Instead, diners would eat as their main dish whatever the chef had prepared. The unpretentious restaurant attracted many patrons of the arts and theater and is remembered as the place were Chicago attorney Paul Harris launched the idea of the Rotary Club in 1905. After Galli died in 1915, her daughter-in-law America Galli took over the restaurant, which moved to Rush Street and, later, to Chicago Avenue. It's not known how long the restaurant survived, but certainly into the '60s.

Colosimo's

Another remarkable Italian restaurant was Colosimo's at 2128 South Wabash Avenue, in the depraved Levee District. In the early 1900s, Gangster "Big Jim" Colosimo opened a café at Archer Street and Armour Avenue (now Federal Street). It did well but became regarded as a hangout for thugs and prostitutes. Perhaps to project a more respectable persona, Colosimo wanted a nicer place, so in 1910, he opened the lavish Colosimo's, with fine food, entertainment and even a rising stage. He took pride in his restaurant, and the food and wine were top-notch. The menu boasted, "One million, five hundred thousand yards of spaghetti always on hand."

Initially, entertainment there featured honkytonk piano and scantily clad dancing girls. But as Colosimo advanced in the world, he provided more reputable entertainment and attracted a more refined clientele. "At the peak of its popularity, the restaurant drew large crowds," Arthur Bilek wrote in *The First Vice Lord*. "Customers include Clarence Darrow, Marshall Field, Potter Palmer and scores of Lake Shore Drive millionaires and North Shore socialites."

And yet Colosimo's was widely recognized as a center of criminal activity. Gambling was always available, just out of sight on the second floor, and all sorts of relationships were formed and deals struck on the first floor. Colosimo ran several brothels, was friends with crooked aldermen, extorted money from local businesses and became the founder of the Chicago Outfit.

Many of Colosimo's cohorts, however, considered the restaurant a distraction from their true calling. In 1920, as part of a gangland power struggle, Colosimo was wacked right inside his own restaurant. His funeral was a huge affair, attracting saloonkeepers and brothel owners, as well as congressmen, judges, federal and state prosecutors, park commissioners and ten aldermen—all as pallbearers and honorary pallbearers! Tens of thousands of mourners lined the streets of the funeral procession in what became the first of many large, flamboyant gangster send-offs.

After Colosimo died, the restaurant became just "another nightlife center," Drury wrote in 1931. "The food and entertainment are on a par with those of other nightclubs. You won't get shot there and…Capone is never seen in the place." Nevertheless, the connection between Colosimo's and organized crime stuck, and the restaurant continued to attract people who were fascinated by its sordid past. The restaurant did not close until 1953. Still, in 1958 when the building was about to be razed, the site was overrun with more than a thousand souvenir hunters.

Como Inn

Como Inn was family oriented—in a different sense of the word. Opened in 1924 at 546 North Milwaukee Avenue, this celebrated restaurant offered high-quality food—course after course—in a dark, intimate setting reminiscent of a Romanesque villa. Some of its cozy booths did not discourage cuddling. The massive structure had majestic hallways lined with marble that connected fourteen rooms. Seating seven hundred, Como Inn was adept at handling banquets, business meetings, large family gatherings and meetings of professional associations. A host of Italian entertainers, from Luciano Pavarotti to Frank Sinatra, dined here. Yes, Perry Como did, too, but he had no connection to the restaurant.

The massive Como Inn could handle a party of two or hundreds of diners. It was dark and richly decorated to resemble a Romanesque villa. *Author's collection.*

The Como Inn offered good value for the money and catered to local businesses and working people for most of its early history. Little by little, however, area businesses closed, and the residential population dwindled. In 1992, the Chicago Transit Authority closed its "L" station at Grand Avenue, a sign of how far the neighborhood had deteriorated. Nevertheless, the Como Inn stayed open, a steady force in a changing neighborhood. Soon, the "L" station reopened and new housing construction began. Regrettably, Como Inn shut its doors in 2001, just when the neighborhood's renaissance was picking up steam.

Bronsky fondly remembers the Como Inn's legendary Festa Dinners. A menu from the '50s describes the affair in this way: "It's Festa Time! Here in a romantic old Italian atmosphere, you may further transport yourself in body and soul by participating in this sumptuous leisurely repast."

Club El Bianco

Even better known than the Como Inn for "Fiesta Dinners" was Club El Bianco (2747 West Sixty-Third Street). These legendary feasts "served in a manner befitting festive royalty of old," as the ads put it, included seven to ten seemingly endless courses, with a scoop of sherbet in the middle of the meal to clear the palate. In addition, colorful rolling carts circulated, piled high with olives, cheese, bread, salad, fruits, nuts and pastries. "The food just kept coming and coming," said Mimi Ferrara, who dined there frequently in

Humphrey Bogart (*center*), Keenan Wynn and an unidentified woman dine at Club El Bianco on the Southwest Side. *Rotunno Family Collection.*

the '50s and '60s and called it Chicago's premier Italian restaurant. "If you were there for less than three hours, it was a miracle."

The chefs called the cooking Northern Italian, but the owners were Sicilian. In any event, the restaurant had a reputation for mob connections. El Bianco, with its crowded, busy atmosphere and rustic Italian décor, advertised that it was "founded on the conviction that every meal should be a special occasion." It stayed open until the '70s.

Another long-standing Italian restaurant was Papa Milano, a small chain that survived for at least sixty years. The original restaurant opened in 1933 in a small house at Clark Street and Diversey Parkway. In 1951, the chain's best-known location opened at 951 North State Street. It was a small informal restaurant that featured good but unimaginative home-style Italian food. Still, Papa Milano was credited with introducing Chicagoans to lasagna, and for that we will be forever grateful.

Riccardo's

One of Chicago's legendary Italian steakhouses, Riccardo's Restaurant and Gallery (437 North Rush Street), was as well known for drinking as for eating. (This once prompted a diner to proclaim, "I'm shocked, shocked, to find that eating is going on here." Of course, that's a reference to the movie *Casablanca* and Rick's nightclub, to which Riccardo's was often compared.)

Riccardo's (aka Ric's) opened in a former speakeasy in 1934, soon after Prohibition ended. Founder Ric Riccardo Sr. was a painter, so he decorated the stucco walls and ceilings of his restaurant with paintings and murals. Some of the works were painted by him, others by important artists—including Ivan Albright and Aaron Bohrad—and still others by local artists hoping for a sale or at least some exposure. A large leather-covered bar shaped like a palette furthered the art theme.

The restaurant/bar became a gathering place for "artists, writers, journalists, opera singers and movie stars, admen, drunks, scalawags and bon vivants, real and would-be," wrote *Tribune* columnist Rick Kogan, who was known to hang out there on occasion. "It was dark in the way all good saloons are dark," Kogan wrote. "Thirsty and ink-stained men and women would congregate at this 'Montmartre of the Midwest.'" Ric's was once the only downtown restaurant to serve blacks "without a hassle," he added.

Some of those journalists sipping Manhattans and martinis at Ric's came in handy in 1943 when Riccardo Sr. was trying to sell Chicago on a new kind of pizza. Legend has it that he and distillery executive Ike Sewell created deep dish pizza, in part because during World War II, flour was more available than the other ingredients typically used to make pizza. They opened Riccardo's Pizzeria in the basement of an old mansion at 29 East Ohio Street, but their thick-crust pizza did not catch on. The restaurant was on the verge of closing when deep dish pizza started getting some favorable reviews from those journalists eating and drinking at Ric's.

When Riccardo Sr. died in 1954, his flamboyant son took over the restaurant. The son, "who was more interested in theater than food service, didn't run the place very well," said the *Tribune*. "Over the years, Ric's slipped as flashy themed restaurants began to take hold." In 1974, Riccardo Jr. sold out to Nick and Bill Angelos, who did an admirable job trying to preserve Ric's original character. At the same time, nearby newspapers were downsizing or closing, which cut into the restaurant's clientele and allure. In addition, customers just stopped drinking so much. Ric's closed in 1995 to tears and toasts from many of its admirers. It morphed into Phil Stefani's 437 Rush, another Italian steakhouse, but this one closed, too, in 2016.

Other Italian Standouts

Café Angelo (225 North Wabash Avenue) stood out because of Angelo Nicelli, its colorful owner, chef, maître d'—and gardener, who grew his own herbs and specialty vegetables. This talented character was also a Broadway song-and-dance man, appearing in such hits as *Oklahoma!* and *Carousel* before moving to Chicago in 1952. Nicelli opened his restaurant in 1970 and, through charm and willpower, kept it going until he turned seventy. He knew many movie stars and politicians, some of whom dropped in frequently. "It's ironic that Angelo's is closing as the Loop is making a comeback," said the *Tribune* when the restaurant closed in 1977. But this was the kind of restaurant that would not have been the same without its founder.

Carlucci (2215 North Halsted Street) opened in 1984 and was one of the first in a new wave of fine Italian restaurants in Chicago that has stretched all the way to today, with the world-class Spiaggia currently holding the top spot. Carlucci was a trendy, high-end restaurant. Some patrons remember it for its month-long Garlic Festival, launched in 1988. Diners could start with a "gartini" cocktail and "garlamari" squid, followed by garlic soup, garlic salad and garlic-stuffed veal rolls. Dessert? You guessed it: roasted garlic dipped in chocolate. Despite this contribution to olfactory history, Carlucci closed in 1997 and moved to the suburbs.

The Carlucci Restaurant Group also ran Strega Nona (3747 North Southport Avenue), a decidedly nontraditional Italian eatery that opened in 1995. If the name sounds odd, *strega nonna* means "grandmother witch" and refers to the eponymous children's stories about a kindly old woman who owns a magical pasta pot. The magic didn't work long for Strega Nona, as this fun, colorfully decorated restaurant closed in the early 2000s.

Bice Ristorante (10 East Delaware Place) was another lively, trendy favorite. This upmarket chain originated in Milan in 1926 and had a warm, dark-wood bar area, with framed fashion sketches lining its walls.

The cozy La Bocca Della Verita (4618 North Lincoln Avenue) offered fresh ingredients, individually prepared dishes and many menu items not available in other Italian restaurants. This included such treats as shrimp with artichokes and not-necessarily-attractive-to-look-at boiled octopus. When Jane Swanson Nystrom ordered the latter, her husband, Doug Nystrom, propped up his menu to hide the bare-looking octopus while he ate his dinner.

Chicago once had more than twenty Italian neighborhoods, all full of ethnic eateries. Today, many Italian restaurants continue to thrive in the three remaining Little Italys: Taylor Street on the West Side; Grand Avenue on the North Side; and Twenty-Fourth Street and Oakley Avenue. Among the most priceless is Bruna's Ristorante (2424 South Oakley Avenue), opened in 1933. The ambiance and menu at this traditional restaurant seem frozen in time. This is the grand dame of Oakley Street, and its delicious dishes (penne puttanesca, chicken vesuvio, shrimp fra diavola) are thoroughly vetted and carefully prepared.

The popular Italian Village (71 West Monroe Street) opened in 1927, even before Bruna's did, and is also still open. The owners have referred to their three-floor establishment as the "General Motors of Italian restaurants": economical Chevrolet downstairs in La Cantina; expensive Buick upstairs in The Village; and luxury Cadillac on the first floor in the Florentine Room (Vivere, since 1990). Although dwarfed by skyscrapers all around, this family-run business shows no signs of letting up or of giving up its valuable real estate.

CHINESE

Of all the Asian cuisines that can be enjoyed in Chicago, Chinese food is most notable in terms of longevity and the number of restaurants. Although Americanized, Chinese food has long been one of the most popular, ubiquitous and affordable ethnic cuisines here.

Chinese began immigrating to Chicago as early as the 1870s. Many who had worked on railroad construction in the West came seeking better jobs—and better treatment. Naturally, these immigrants brought their food preferences and cooking habits with them, which motivated Chinese immigrants to build restaurants. In fact, the food industry was one of the few areas of business open to them.

So many immigrants arrived that by 1900, there were an estimated 100 to 150 Chinese restaurants in Chicago, almost all of them Chinese owned. These restaurants became a channel to success for the entire community. In addition to making money, feeding their fellow compatriots and introducing Chinese food to Americans, these restaurants provided generations of Chinese Americans with the opportunity to own a business and to employ family and friends. The area near Clark and Van Buren Streets developed into Chicago's first Chinatown, but early Chinese restaurants were found throughout downtown.

Many early Chinese restaurants were palatial and located downtown. King Joy Lo claimed, justifiably so, to be the world's "Finest Chinese American Restaurant." *Eric Bronsky.*

While some of these restaurants were so-called chop suey joints, others were lavish, even regal affairs, catering to businessmen and travelers. The three-story King Joy Lo (57 West Randolph Street) opened in 1906 or 1907 and was nothing short of fabulous. It featured inlaid teakwood, carved pagodas, mirrored walls, massive columns decorated with carved lotus flowers and a mosaic fountain in the rotunda under a chandelier with one thousand lights. Such features allowed King Joy Lo to unabashedly claim to be the "Finest Chinese American Restaurant in the World."

King Joy Lo's eight-page menus—one for Chinese fare and another for American—were equally ornate and impressive. Its multiple kitchens, including one just for cooking rice, were "open to public inspection at any time." On opening night, "hundreds of well-dressed men and women crowded around the entrance, clamoring for admittance," according to the *Tribune*. "Such a sight never before was seen in Chicago."

King Joy Lo was started by the Empire Reform Association to raise funds to support its work in China, i.e., supporting the emperor. To raise more money, manager Chin Foin targeted affluent Americans and used Western plates and cutlery. Disposition of the profits became a thorny issue, but this apparently did not compromise the quality of the food and service.

In the early 1900s, Chinese food was new to many Chicagoans, so much so that King Joy Lo's menu went to great lengths explaining things. On how to share food, for example, it said, "Instead of individual orders, if a party of four orders a variety of single dishes…a really pretentious spread may be secured at a trifling expense." Since the restaurant stood across the street from the Garrick Theater, it was a popular spot to gather after performances. King Joy Lo thrived until the '40s.

In 1911, Chin Foin went on to open the Mandarin Inn (414 South Wabash Avenue), a fancy place that featured a pipe organ with daily concerts. He followed this in 1919 with the New Mandarin Inn, also on Wabash. His restaurants were increasingly Americanized, the last one using table linens and serving European wine.

Chin Foin's restaurants, as well as other lavish Chinese palace restaurants such as the Oriental Inn, were large and memorable. Hoe Sai Gai (75 West Randolph Street) was particularly imposing. From the '30s to the '60s, this top-flight restaurant sported a huge, ostentatious marquee and attracted big-name entertainers.

The development of the Loop drove up rents and property values, eventually pushing Chinese restaurants, small and large, out of downtown to a neighborhood around Twenty-Second Street and Wentworth Avenue, which became Chicago's traditional Chinatown. The casual restaurants

Opposite, top: Hoe Sai Gai, another lavish Chinese restaurant in the Loop, flourished from the '30s until the '60s. Its huge marquee lit up the street. *Eric Bronsky.*

Opposite, bottom: The stunning Hoe Sai Gai regaled diners with excellent Cantonese food and a spectacular well-designed Art Deco interior. *Eric Bronsky.*

opened there would never match the opulence of the early mesmerizing Chinese restaurants downtown.

Another significant Chinese eatery was the Pekin House (2311 West Devon Avenue), which opened in the '50s and closed in 2012. This long run could be attributed to its egg rolls (prepared with peanut butter), which generated an almost cult-like following.

The popular Jimmy Wong's (426 South Wabash Avenue) was also launched in the '50s and known for Cantonese cooking, Hong Kong steak and whole-fish dishes, as well as for celebrity sightings, at least in its early years. Wong was called "Mr. Restaurateur," and he went all out to welcome diners. The food was plentiful and affordable, including such delicacies as chicken wrapped roll, butterfly shrimp, Chinese barbecued ribs, Manchu steak and king-sized white fried shrimp. And those were just a few of the appetizers. The two-floor restaurant often won high marks with Chicagoans, but that may have been because it "lived up to Westerners' expectations of a Chinese restaurant," said the *Tribune* in 1979. This included Oriental waiters in flowered shirts, a pagoda-like skylight and a bubbling Buddha fountain. Plus, the food was "commercial Chinese" rather than traditional. Still, it was a successful formula, and Wong opened another restaurant of the same name at 3058 West Peterson Avenue. The downtown one closed in 1997.

Ben Pao (52 West Illinois Street) was Lettuce Entertain You's first foray into Chinese cuisine. The pricey but popular place operated from 1996 to 2011 and featured a tea bar and a ritzy dining area.

But most remembered of all is Won Kow (2237 South Wentworth Avenue). Opened in 1928, it was Chicago's oldest continuously operating

This 1968 menu made the unusual claim of being Chicago's "most publicized Chinese restaurant," with one Jimmy Wong's downtown and another on Peterson Avenue. *Chicago History Museum.*

Chinese restaurant—until it closed in 2018. That left the modest Orange Garden (1942 West Irving Park Road) as the oldest. Orange Garden serves, quite simply, good food at reasonable prices. It shows that good Chinese restaurants were (and still are) sprinkled all over town. In 1931, Drury described the Orange Garden thus: "Not just another chop suey parlor, but truly Chinese…as Chinese as your laundry slip in cuisine, appointments and clientele."

Meanwhile, a second Chinatown began forming in Uptown in the '60s. It was a dream of Wong's, and initial plans called for a mall with restaurants, shops, pagodas, fountains and trees. Wong never realized this vision, but the New Chinatown (aka Little Saigon) is inviting and includes mainly Vietnamese restaurants, as well as Thai, Korean, Laotian and Cambodian cookeries.

SWEDISH

Swedes are not numerous in Chicago today, but historically they represented a large and influential immigrant group, especially during the twentieth century. "We built the city," said Doug Nystrom, a Swedish resident of North Park, which, along with Andersonville, is one of the two Scandinavian enclaves still active in the city. He may have been exaggerating a bit, but constructing Wrigley Field and the Wrigley Building, as the Swedes did, must have built up some serious appetites. That would explain the disproportionately large number of Swedish restaurants in Chicago over the years.

One of the most prominent was Villa Sweden (5207 North Clark Street), renowned for its smorgasbord, a twice-weekly, hours-long, all-you-can-eat affair that cost only $2.25 in 1959 and $4.25 in 1978. It was loaded with Swedish specialties, including herring, lutefisk, meatballs, limpa bread, brown beans…and lingonberries galore. Olga Beckman opened this attractive restaurant in the '30s, making it one of the few women-owned eateries in Chicago at the time. And she emphasized in advertisements that she was genuinely Swedish. The *Tribune* described Villa Sweden as having "a starchy blue-and-white décor…[with] tearoom primness and well-modulated conversation." Alcohol was not served at this pristine place.

One block north, House of Sweden (5314 North Clark Street) competed with Villa Sweden. Both were beautifully decorated for the holidays and particularly affordable. "Lots for less," as the *Tribune* put it, something that

NIELSEN'S RESTAURANT
UNSURPASSED SMÖRGÅSBORD

Above: Most Swedish restaurants offered sumptuous smorgasbords like this one at Nielsen's (7330 West North Avenue). *Author's collection.*

Right: This 1959 menu cover for A Bit of Sweden, one of many fine Swedish restaurants, suggests propriety and national pride. *Chicago History Museum.*

ca. 1959

A
Bit
of
Sweden

Skål!!

1015 North Rush Street ♦ Chicago 11, Illinois

the supposedly parsimonious Swedes must have appreciated. Meanwhile, A Bit of Sweden had its own charm. It opened at 1015 Rush Street prior to 1931 and moved to 104 East Walton Street, where it lasted into the '60s. Diners recall a quaint atmosphere, generous smorgasbord and delicious food, as well as blond waitresses in costume.

Kungsholm Puppet Opera

Most famous of all the Swedish restaurants was Kungsholm (100 East Ontario Street) in the magnificent 1890s McCormick family mansion, with winding staircases, attractive woodwork and stately fireplaces. This restaurant was known for its sumptuous smorgasbord, heavily laden with Swedish meatballs, pancakes, Danish rum pudding and a large number of fish items, including pickled eel, anchovy aspic and, of course, several varieties of herring.

Despite the abundance of delicious food, some of which was exotic to non-Scandinavians, Kungsholm is best remembered for its Miniature Grand Puppet Opera. Ernest Wolff launched this intricate puppet show in 1936. The following year, he installed it in a ballroom of the mansion as part of the newly established Kungsholm Restaurant. Diners describe the show as enchanting. It used beautifully costumed puppets in an attractive,

Kungsholm served excellent food but is most fondly remembered for its Miniature Grand Puppet Opera. *Lawry's The Prime Rib.*

Kungsholm puppets performed full operas. The most popular were *Carmen*, *La Traviata*, *Rigoletto* and *Madame Butterfly*. *Lawry's The Prime Rib.*

craftily lit miniature theater. The articulated rod puppets were operated from beneath the stage, as opposed to marionettes, which are operated from above. (Therefore, there were "no strings attached.") Vinyl records provided the music, but a few famous operatic performers, including Mario Lanza, Jeanette MacDonald and Lauritz Melchior, sang here in person. The enthralling performances introduced some young people to a lifelong love of opera.

In 1957, the Fred Harvey restaurant chain purchased Kungsholm, and things went downhill from there. The restaurant and show closed in 1971, and the puppets were donated to the Museum of Science and Industry. That same year, however, Opera in Focus revived the art of puppet opera and still performs extravagant scenes from various operas at the Rolling Meadows Park District Theater.

In 1976, Lawry's The Prime Rib took over Kungsholm's space and today features prime rib, carved tableside, as well as its famous, often copied, spinning salad bowl.

A few Swedish restaurants keep memories alive today. There were once three Ann Sather restaurants in Chicago, and the original one (909 West Belmont Avenue) remains popular, especially for breakfast. The tiny diner Svea (5236 North Clark Street) reminds Chicagoans that Andersonville was once dominated by Swedish residents and businesses. And Tre Kronor (3258 West Foster Avenue) carries on Scandinavian traditions in the alluring North Park community, serving up genuine traditional cuisines and experiences, most notably with its extensive Christmas julbord.

RUSSIAN

Relatively few Russians moved to Chicago, so there's been a dearth of such restaurants. One of the best was Sasha's Russian (914 Ernst Court), opened in 1957. The intimate baronial-style place specialized in imperial Russian cuisine. It was quite successful, despite Cold War tensions, perhaps because its Russian-born owner and chef, Alexander "Sasha" Vereschagin, talked about how he "fled the commies with a loud lusty 'nyet-for-me,'" according to a *Tribune* column about the restaurant's tenth anniversary. The colorful bearded owner was known as a great cook, singer and storyteller.

Diners at Sasha's devoured copious amounts of food—borscht, chicken Kiev, caviar, et cetera, all washed down with jaw-dropping amounts of vodka. The restaurant was known for delicious hearty soups, including "Shut Up and Eat It" soup. When customers asked what was in the tasty potage, Vereschagin, creator of some two hundred different soup recipes, would simply say, "Shut up and eat it."

Patrons were probably better off not knowing what was in Sasha's strong drinks, either. Restaurant critics warned customers to beware of the Czarina, a cocktail of Cointreau, lemon juice and vodka served over crushed ice. At a luncheon for the Woman's Board of the Field Museum, Vereschagin urged his customers to try a mixture of vodka and Cherry Heering liquor. "It's called a 'Red Russian,' and I invented it fifteen minutes ago!" he said. A trip to Sasha's was more like going to a party than eating at a restaurant. But

A few Russian restaurants, including Moscow at Night, offered borscht, chicken Kiev and caviar, as well as vodka flights. *Robert Krueger photo. Chicago Public Library, Northside Neighborhood History Collection.*

Vereschagin did not reopen his restaurant after a fire destroyed it in the early '70s. Instead, he went the piano-bar route.

Other closed but memorable Russian restaurants include Moscow at Night on the corner of Peterson and Albany Avenues and Bratislava (2527 North Clark Street). Today, the elegant Russian Tea Time (17 East Adams Street), beautifully decorated with samovars and fresh-cut flowers, serves authentic Russian food and a delightful afternoon tea.

MEXICAN

Café Azteca (210 West North Avenue), one of Chicago's earliest Mexican restaurants, opened in 1957 when Old Town was dreary by day and deserted by night. Before urban renewal drove it out, the small but charming restaurant offered a tasty selection of Mexican dishes and introduced many Chicagoans to what they considered an exotic cuisine. Café Azteca also attracted attention with its *posada*, a traditional ritual that reenacts Mary and Joseph's search for lodging.

La Hacienda del Sol (1945 North Sedgwick Street) further confirms that the Near North Side hosted a vibrant Hispanic community in the '60s, a time when a growing number of cantinas were replacing bierstubes. And nearby, El Grifon, a Cuban restaurant on the second floor of 1529 North

cafe
AZTECA
II
1977

Café Azteca (210 West North Avenue) opened in 1957, back when Old Town was home to many Hispanic restaurants. *Chicago History Museum.*

Wells Street, started in 1960 as a showcase for an interior decorator transplanted from Cuba. The fried bananas, black beans and rice he served as refreshments turned out to be so popular with his customers that Hacienda del Sol was born.

Fernando's (3450 North Lincoln Avenue) was known for its year-round patio, as the tables and brightly colored umbrellas were brought indoors for the winter. Patrons also appreciated the many regional dishes offered along with the mainstream Mexican menu. Other noteworthy Mexican restaurants that dated back to the '60s include Carta Blanca, La Margarita, Su Casa, Acapulco and Mexico Lindo.

More contemporary and less traditional was Hat Dance (325 West Huron Street) opened in 1988 by Lettuce Entertain You in partnership with radio celebrity Steve Dahl (famous for Disco Demolition Night at Comiskey Park in 1979). This classy, distinctive restaurant served creative, beautifully plated dishes, such as queso fundido, fajitas, adobado and guacamole made from sweet peas. The restaurant also had a Japanese flavor, serving sushi and sake margaritas, both novelties. The trendy restaurant was a great place for people-watching, but the buzz did not last. It was replaced in 1999 by Nacional 27, a pan-Hispanic concept—twenty-seven being the number of Latino nations represented on the restaurant's menu.

IRISH

Despite the huge number of Irish immigrants that made Chicago home, this group built and patronized few memorable restaurants. Some experts explain this by pointing out that for Irish Americans, the center of life outside home—other than the church—was the pub, where food was not the primary purpose. Furthermore, while the German bierstube, Polish tavern and Mexican cantina were full of families, especially on Sundays, the Irish pub was primarily patronized by men. Also, the Irish cuisine is not as rich and varied as that of other nationalities. Perhaps, too, Irish immigrants pursued other avenues to advancement: politics, police work and the priesthood.

That said, the Irish American cuisine entails more than boiled potatoes and Guinness, as some will joke. It includes delicious standards such as shepherd's pie, corned beef and cabbage, cheddar cheese soup and fish and chips. All of these treats could be found at the popular Grace O'Malley's Restaurant & Pub (1416 South Michigan Avenue). Its proximity to Grant Park and Soldier Field made O'Malley's a popular spot for pre-concert and pre-game meals. The food was a cut above typical pub grub, and the décor was warm and inviting, with a beautiful wood bar in front.

Other old-time Irish eateries that have come and gone include Cullen's Bar & Grill (3741 North Southport Avenue), a friendly place that closed in 2015; Connolly's Tavern (1445 West Devon Avenue); McGuigans Irish Pub (3358 North Ashland Avenue); McFaden's Restaurant and Saloon (1206 North State Parkway); and Moher Public House (5310 West Devon Avenue). For a genuine Irish pub today, check out the Irish Oak (3511 North Clark Street) or Kitty O'Shea's (720 South Michigan Avenue), both with décor largely imported from the Emerald Isle. In any event, Chicago never experienced a shortage of "Irish" restaurants on St. Patrick's Day.

JAPANESE

Mrs. Shintani's (originally at 3725 South Lake Park Avenue) was one of Chicago's earliest Japanese restaurants, although dates are not known. In 1931, Drury described the restaurant as "exotic," noting that it specialized in sukiyaki, prepared tableside. That year, Prince and Princess Takamatsu ate at Mrs. Shintani's during their honeymoon. In 1934, the restaurant moved to a house on Rush Street, and a *Tribune* reporter who dined there in 1937 noted that Japanese restaurants were known for giving patrons their unfinished food to take home in a bag. This is surprising because the origin of the doggie bag is often pegged to World War II. Mrs. Shintani's was briefly closed by police due to the owner's nationality after Pearl Harbor was bombed.

The first Japanese restaurant thought to cater to non-Japanese patrons was Wisteria Tea Room (212 East Ohio Street). It was opened in the

Japanese restaurants have waxed and waned in Chicago. The Naka-No-Ya was popular in the '50s and '60s. *Author's collection.*

mid-'40s by Mrs. Okimoto, one of the first of more than thirty thousand Japanese Americans to leave a U.S. government relocation camp and settle in Chicago. A 1944 ad does not describe Wisteria as Japanese, which is not surprising given the war, but it does say it is "the only restaurant in Chicago serving sukiyaki." It's not known how long this restaurant remained open.

One of the most iconic Japanese restaurants was the Azuma Sukiyaki House. It opened in the late '50s in a former Schlitz tied house at 5120 North Broadway and lasted into the '90s. The historic building currently houses the South-East Asia Center.

The elegant and expensive Naka-No-Ya (2100 North Lincoln Park West) was highly regarded from the late '50s until it closed in 1973. Early ads for this classic restaurant invited people to "dine in the unique and exotic environment of 'Sayonara' and 'Teahouse of the August Moon,'" two highly publicized movies released in the '50s (both of which, coincidentally, star Marlon Brando).

The Japanese/Hawaiian Diamond Head restaurant (3321 West Columbus Avenue) was popular during the '60s and '70s. "From the moment one walks into the restaurant to the soft strains of oriental music, a calm and relaxed mood is at hand and remains with you throughout the dinner," said a reviewer in 1963.

Where Cooking is an Art . . .
. . . And Service a Pleasure

Nankin Chinese Foods are
Famous for Balanced Rations

66 West Randolph St.
Chicago

15 South Seventh St.
Minneapolis

A menu cover from Nanking (66 West Randolph Street) is very inviting. It oozes elegance and good taste but with a touch of the exotic. *Chicago History Museum.*

These Japanese restaurants are remembered for kimono-clad waitresses, Tatami rooms and dishes prepared tableside on Hibachi stoves, not to mention the miso soup, teriyaki, tempura and sake. As a concession to Americans who were not used to sitting on the floor, virtually all these restaurants had wells beneath their low tables for legs and feet. Especially extravagant was Benihana (166 East Superior Street), where "dinner and a show" took on a whole new meaning. Knife-flipping chefs would slice and dice your meal tableside.

More recently, celebrity chef Masaharu Morimoto opened Japonais by Morimoto in 2003 at 600 West Chicago Avenue in the old Montgomery Ward warehouse. This excellent, chic restaurant quickly became one of the "buzziest" places in town. It had a swanky indoor-outdoor layout that overlooked the North Branch of the Chicago River. Japonais was hailed as "a culinary marvel of the new millennium" and credited with "the infusion of Japanese cuisine with European elegance…with a hint of the contemporary." It closed in 2015 due to a dispute about back rent.

ROMANIAN

Joe Stein's Original Roumanian Restaurant dates back to about 1900 in the Maxwell Street area. It moved a couple of times before settling in at 5356 North Sheridan Road, where it survived until 1980. Fondly remembered for strolling gypsy musicians, it served hearty vegetable-barley soup, roasted duck, tender sweetbreads, stuffed cabbage and luscious walnut strudel.

Diners also remember the Romanian restaurant Little Bucharest at 3001 North Ashland Avenue, an unlikely location, but the small place was charming. Opened in 1970, Little Bucharest was known for hefty portions of delicious food. At some point, the quality slipped but then rebounded. "New ownership seems to be bringing this faded favorite back to its glory days of the seventies, with staggering portions…and homemade desserts," the *Tribune* wrote in 1991. "Appetizers are big enough for entrees, and entrees overlap the big plates."

Chicago was sorry to lose this eatery for a few years but pleased to see it reopen in 2009 as Little Bucharest Bistro at 3661 North Elston Avenue. Branko Podrumedic, the past and current owner, is known for running the annual Taste of Romania street festival. At the lively new restaurant,

Here in 1981, Little Bucharest was in Lakeview. This popular Romanian restaurant later moved to 3661 North Elston Avenue, where it continues to entertain diners. *Robert Krueger photo. Chicago Public Library, Northside Neighborhood History Collection.*

which is decorated with stained-glass windows and offers sidewalk seating, Podrumedic serves a liquor he calls "holy water," roasts a lamb or pig on a spit outside for Sunday brunch and regularly features live music.

OTHER ETHNIC RESTAURANTS

Chicago has seen so many ethnic restaurants come and go that this book can't begin to cover them all, but here are a few more.

One favorite was Gandhi India (26012 West Devon Avenue), appreciated for its wide variety of curries and other delightfully seasoned dishes. Another popular place was House of India (1743 North Wells Street). Today, the Viceroy of India continues that tradition. Also still operating are Gaylord India Restaurant and the Bombay Palace, both of which introduced many Chicagoans to Indian and Pakistani cuisine starting in the '70s.

Salaam (8300 South Cottage Grove Avenue) was a Muslim restaurant that opened during the '70s and distinguished itself by serving no pork and never allowing smoking.

An often-remembered Hungarian restaurant was the unpretentious Epicurean (316 South Wabash Avenue), where diners enjoyed beef goulash and chicken paprikash. Especially notable was the flight of strudel, a heavenly assortment of different flavors.

CHAPTER 9

African American Restaurants

African American restaurants date back to Chicago's early days but blossomed with the first wave of the Great Migration starting in the 1910s. Back then, the cuisine was known as down-home, country or southern cooking, and it grew rapidly in popularity in Chicago as the African American population grew here, primarily though migration from the South. By 1923, a directory printed in the *Chicago Defender*, an influential African American newspaper, listed one hundred black-owned restaurants. They were concentrated, however, in the "Black Belt," a narrow corridor along State Street on the South Side that confined African American residents—and restaurants.

Down-home restaurants served such treats as barbecue ribs, smothered chicken, black-eyed peas, corn bread, rice and beans, biscuits, cobbler and sweet potato pie, all of which were typically made from scratch. But reflecting the roots in poverty and slavery, this cuisine also included many dishes that were based on food that slaveholders would have thrown out, including greens, chitterlings, fat back, cow brains, oxtails and pigs' feet, ears and tails. The cooks made these rejected ingredients into not only palatable but decidedly delicious dishes.

A yearning for southern-style cooking—and not being welcome in or even served at other types of restaurants—led African Americans to open and patronize their own restaurants. In his 1931 *Dining in Chicago*, John Drury mentioned only three African American restaurants: Duck Inn, Chapman's and Poro Tea Room. They were all in a part of town that has

Waitresses at the Soul Queen Café pose for a City 2000 photo. Behind them is a photo of owner Helen Maybell with Muhammad Ali. *Jon Lowenstein photo.*

become known as Bronzeville, and they're all long gone. Ironically, Poro operated from an imposing gray stone mansion at 4415 South Park Way (now Martin Luther King Drive) that had been built for John R. Thompson, the founder of a nationwide chain of cafeterias that refused to serve African Americans, according to Jan Whitaker of the authoritative Restaurant-ing Through History blog. It took numerous lawsuits over decades to reverse that despicable practice.

The second wave of the Great Migration running from 1945 to 1970 expanded the Black Belt, and eventually broke out of its limits. This led to the presence of African American residents and restaurants throughout Chicago. Such eateries came to represent black culture and opened other Chicagoans to this distinctive cuisine. They embodied culinary traditions and nourished the heart and soul—as much as did black churches, community centers and barbershops—of the African American communities they served.

LEGENDARY ARMY & LOU'S

Among the most popular black restaurants from this era was Army & Lou's, first at Thirty-Ninth Street and Indiana Avenue and from the '70s on at 422 East Seventy-Fifth Street. Given its striking neon sign, the restaurant was quite visible and easily recognized from afar. William "Army" Armstrong, an employee of the crusading black newspaper *Chicago Defender*, and his wife, Louvella, opened this restaurant in 1945. It was relatively small but served up large portions of delicious "soul food with style," as the owners put it. It offered a fine dining atmosphere, with linen napkins and tablecloth, as well as rotating art exhibits, and was frequented by middle-class patrons, both black and white.

The family-oriented restaurant was a well-established and highly regarded dining destination, with jazz nights, Sunday buffets and what many called "the best fried chicken anywhere." Nevertheless, after an incredible run of sixty-five years (with a temporary closure starting in 1992), Army & Lou's closed for good in 2010 due to a lack of patronage, poor economy and deteriorating neighborhood conditions. In addition, its physical space was in need of a serious overhaul. After it closed, another owner tried to revive the establishment but failed about a year later.

Another celebrated African American restaurant, Gladys' Luncheonette (4527 South Indiana Avenue), was founded by Gladys Holcomb a few years after she moved to Chicago from the South in 1946. The small place was comfortable but not fancy, with a counter running alongside the dining room. It was known as a hangout for musicians of many stripes. Holcomb built her reputation not only on her great, fluffy biscuits (which are much more difficult to master than one might think) but, more importantly, on opening up her restaurant to the community. She posted church announcements, obituaries of patrons and stellar report cards of neighborhood schoolchildren. She promoted local events and publicized community news. And she patronized black arts and displayed sculptures of local artists in her luncheonette. Holcomb's eponymous restaurant closed in 2001, and she died in 2003.

Country cooking or southern food fans will also remember Queen of the Sea (aka "The Q") at 7611 South Stony Island Avenue. This large but plain restaurant had four separate dining rooms and a bar. Patrons could grab a plate and eat as much as they liked from the copious buffet. H&H Restaurant (1425 West Eighty-Seventh Street) also offered a buffet. Its jukebox played gospel and rhythm and blues hits. Meanwhile, the Coffee Cup Restaurant (7100 South Jeffrey Avenue) treated diners to forty-six kinds of chili. (Take that, Cincinnati!)

SOUL FOOD TAKES CENTER STAGE

By the time of the civil rights movement in the '50s and '60s, down-home southern cooking had become known as "soul food." Several restaurants opened throughout the city to capitalize on the growing interest in this non-mainstream, overlooked style of cooking that had nonetheless contributed so much to American culture and cuisine.

The most fashionable of the new soul food eateries was the Soul Queen Café (2200 South Michigan Avenue), opened in 1970 by the stylish Helen Maybell. She referred to herself as "queen of the realm" and regarded her restaurant as a kingdom where waitresses were referred to as "queens" (as indicated on their name tag), cooks as "royal chefs" and busboys and dishwashers as "princes." The restaurant created a unique version of the traditional Chinese fortune cookie. It placed slips of paper glued to napkins on the tables with sayings that Queen Helen called "food-for-thought." One read, "Common sense is in spite of, not the result of, education." Another read, "An excellent way to cover up a bad past is to build a big future over it." In 1975, Soul Queen Café moved to 9031 South Stony Island Avenue, where it enjoyed a successful run. It closed in 2009 after its flamboyant founder died.

Izola's Family Dining, another soul food restaurant that Chicagoans fondly remember, stood at 522 East Seventy-Ninth Street and was known for seafood. The restaurant was named after Izola White, who moved from Tennessee to Chicago in the '40s by herself at the age of nineteen. The twenty-four-hour diner, with strong ties to Mayor Harold Washington and many other African American politicians, operated from the '50s until 2011. Izola's, which sometimes fed people for free or extended credit, was a community staple. Meanwhile, the House of Lord Church on the South

Side ran a particularly "soulful" restaurant inside its church. Opened in 1968, the restaurant had no prices on its menu; instead, inspirational signs posted around the place asked patrons to pay what they could. One sign said, "Eat out. The wife you save might be your own!"

Many Chicagoans sorely miss Dixie Kitchen & Bait Shop, which opened in 1994 at Fifty-Third Street and Harper Avenue in the multilevel Harper Court shopping center. Despite its contrived décor, this lively southern food mecca served a tantalizing mix of Louisiana-style treats, including johnnycakes, jambalaya, andouille sausage, pulled-pork sandwiches and pecan pie. One of its claims to fame was a 2008 appearance on WTTW's program *Check Please*, in which a young Barack Obama named Dixie Kitchen one of his favorite restaurants. Unfortunately, the shopping center housing this restaurant fell victim to a 2009 redevelopment for a new office and retail tower. The restaurant was never able to fit into or afford the new surroundings. The development, sponsored by the University of Chicago, resulted in accusations of bullying and racism

Perfect Eat Shoppe on Forty-Seventh Street near South Park Way (Martin Luther King Drive) in 1942. At this time, African Americans were not welcome in many Chicago restaurants. *Author's collection.*

against that elite institution. For a while, another Dixie Kitchen operated in Evanston, but it has also closed.

The redevelopment of the Harper Court shopping center also drove out Calypso Café, although not until 2011. Run by the same owners as the Dixie Kitchen, this vibrant, kitschy restaurant opened in 1997 and offered well-crafted tastes of the Caribbean islands, such as black bean soup, plantains, jerk chicken, conch chowder and rice and beans. Diners ate under thatch ceiling fans to the beat of reggae tunes. Harper Court reopened in 2013, and the area houses several restaurants, including Chipotle, Native Foods and McDonald's. These are fine places to eat, if you like chain restaurants, but the Hyde Park community and the whole city lost two unique restaurants through this redevelopment project.

WEST SIDE STORY

Most of Chicago's iconic soul food restaurants were on the South Side, but the West Side could also boast of some legendary establishments. Edna's Soul Food Restaurant opened in 1966 in Austin and later moved to 3175 West Madison Street. It featured fried catfish, short ribs, okra, Arkansas-style biscuits and other classic soul food dishes.

Founder Edna Stewart was famous for many things besides providing traditional, consistently good home-cooked meals. Edna's was a pillar of strength for the West Side, and patrons, neighbors and community organizations looked upon Stewart as a godmother, fairy or otherwise. She served school kids history lessons along with their lunches. She hosted civil rights meetings, most notably those convened by Reverend Martin Luther King Jr. to organize his campaign against housing discrimination in Chicago. In 1989, Stewart was the first to bring soul food to the Taste of Chicago. And she was appreciated for hiring felons recently released from prison when most other enterprises would not consider such a thing.

As a result of Stewart's good works, Governor Pat Quinn declared February 19, 2010, Edna Stewart Day, praising her for "devoting over four decades to serving delicious food and second chances." That same year, Stewart died, and her restaurant closed shortly afterward. The following year, a longtime employee reopened the site as Ruby's Restaurant with many of the same staff members and recipes, but it lasted only one year under the new name and owners.

As well as a restaurant, Edna's Soul Food on the West Side was also a community center, civil rights meeting room and second home to many. *Eric Bronsky*.

Another popular West Side place was Alice's Soul Food at 5638 West Chicago Avenue, but it recently closed after more than thirty years. Meanwhile, in 1988, the Loop got its first major soul food restaurant, Soul by the Pound—$3.99 per pound, to be precise—at 168 North State Street. Owner Otis Taylor reported that some patrons piled their flimsy plastic plates with as much as one and a half pounds of catfish, salmon patties, mac and cheese and other treats. The Chicago Health Department closed this restaurant in 1994 for unsafe food handling practices.

BUILDING COMMUNITY, MAINTAINING TRADITIONS

No matter what side of town they were on, Chicago's southern and soul food restaurants shared more than similar menu items. They were all affordable, and they all provided many black entrepreneurs and employees with jobs. More importantly, they built community, promoted identity and preserved African American traditions.

"It's really about a lot more than the food," said Audria Huntington, who frequently dines out on soul food. "Basically, you have the roots of your culture in the restaurant," he told the *Sun-Times* in 2011. One of the eighty-one-year-old's favorite soul food restaurants was Josephine's Cooking, where he usually ordered the liver and onions or chicken and waffles. (By 2008, Josephine's Cooking had taken over the cherished Captain's Hard Time Dining, a Creole and soul food fixture at 436 East Seventy-Ninth Street.)

Another shared trait of Chicago's African American restaurants is that they were (and still are) popular with politicians at election time. Stopping at these sites, not to mention gulping down grits, gumbo and greens, was de rigueur for any politician hoping to win African American votes. Virtually all politicians would make the rounds.

In addition, most soul food restaurants boasted about serving prominent African Americans, whether politicians (Jesse Jackson and Harold Washington), musicians (James Brown and Smokey Robinson), sports figures (Ernie Banks and Muhammad Ali) or civil rights leaders (Rosa Parks, Martin Luther King Jr. and Nelson Mandela). The photo wall-of-fame at Army & Lou's even included the often overlooked but significant celebrity category of authors (Richard Wright and James Baldwin).

In the past several years, Chicago has lost many of its iconic soul food restaurants as the city's black population continues its long, slow decline. Another factor in the demise of these eateries is changing tastes. Rich, rib-sticking soul food has been criticized for being unhealthy due to its high levels of fat, cholesterol, sugar and salt—and thanks to the typically large portions these restaurants are known for serving. Most soul food restaurants smother, bread or deep-fry much of what's on their menu. While this diet does not necessarily lead to hypertension, obesity and diabetes with everyone, it does contribute to poor health in many people, especially if they lead a sedentary lifestyle. "Soul food restaurants are not a place for dieters," wrote *Tribune* columnist Clarence Page in 1979. Meanwhile, food critics and sociologists argue that the popularity of fast food—indubitably less healthy than soul food—has diminished the appeal of the traditional African American diet.

Still, soul food marches on at the few remaining African American restaurants in Chicago, such as the precious Pearl's Place (3901 South Michigan Avenue) and Soul Vegetarian East (203 East Seventy-Fifth Street). Chicago historian and author Bernard Turner, who specializes in Bronzeville, praises both of these restaurants in his book *Chicago Neighborhoods with Flavor*. Pearl's Place "reinvents a downhome Southern atmosphere in an urban setting," he wrote. Of Soul Vegetarian East, which goes by the tagline "Serving Food as Medicine," Turner writes, "It's hard to imagine eating dishes such as barbecue, roast and gyros that do not contain any meat. The key ingredient is gluten flour, but the real key to the flavor is the seasonings."

Other current soul food choices include Big Jones (5347 North Clark Street) for Cajun boudin fritters, fried green tomatoes and bourbon bread pudding; Miss Lee's Good Food (203 East Garfield Boulevard) for carryout; and MacArthur's (5412 West Madison Street). Visit these remaining authentic eateries. They need your support, and you won't go away hungry.

CHAPTER 10

Themed Restaurants

C hicagoans have long enjoyed playing with their food. They've come up with—and embraced—umpteen casual, carefree and curious restaurants characterized by fun, appealing or novel themes. Gratefully, the Windy City has never seen a Christmas restaurant, like those boutiques that sell Christmas ornaments and Advent calendars year-round. But it has seen restaurants dedicated to exotic cocktails, the Gay Nineties, merry-go-rounds, sports, bicycles, boating and motorcycles. Such themes made the dining experience more memorable, so let's dig in.

TIKI RESTAURANTS

During the mid-twentieth century, tiki-themed bars and restaurants that served strong drinks in a South Seas décor were popular nationwide. The craze started in 1934 when Ernest Gantt opened Beachcomber Café in Hollywood, California. A former bootlegger, Gantt realized that the end of Prohibition would spark the opportunity to serve cocktails in open, elegant settings. He soon changed his name to Donn Beach and renamed his bar Don the Beachcomber.

After the restaurant's rum concoctions proved popular, Beach opened similar restaurants in other cities. Then World War II shined a spotlight on the South Pacific, a remote part of the world previously unexamined

Don the Beachcomber in Hollywood, California, launched the tiki fad in food and drink. It opened a branch in Chicago in 1940. *Eric Bronsky.*

by most Americans. After the war, soldiers returned home with coconut shells, grass skirts, carved wood and other island souvenirs, as well as stories about the islands. Meanwhile, popular culture was celebrating the island culture. James Michener's best-selling *Tales of the South Pacific* was published in 1947. Two years later, the musical adaptation of the book opened on Broadway, and ten years later, the popular musical was made into a movie. Also, Hawaii became a state in 1959. All these factors stimulated curiosity about Pacific islands.

Ultimately, there would be more than fifteen Don the Beachcomber restaurants, including one in Chicago (101 East Walton Street) that opened in 1940. It featured jazzed-up, Americanized Cantonese food, loaded with pineapple and coconut to make it taste or look somewhat tropical. On the menu: rumaki, Chungking shrimp, pork soyo and Mandarin duck. Perhaps most popular was the pupu platter, a combination plate of appetizers.

That said, the elaborate drinks, decorated with little umbrellas and served in pineapple hulls, coconut shells or cups shaped like totem poles, were Don the Beachcomber's biggest attraction. The restaurant in Chicago featured more than eighty kinds of rum that allowed for more than sixty-five original concoctions, including the Mai Tai, Zombie and Missionary's Downfall. Fake rain on the restaurant's tin roof encouraged patrons to stay longer and drink more. After all, the restaurant's motto was "Where good rum is immortalized and drinking is an art."

The quasi Polynesian décor made much use of carved wood masks, palm fronds, rattan furniture, torches and artifacts that might have washed up on a beach. The cluttered mess could have been described as tacky as well as tiki. Still, the public ate it up. One couple, impressed with the décor, told the *Sun-Times* in 1958, "We dined hard by a stalk of bananas hanging from the ceiling, surrounded by bamboo, fish netting and tanks of tropical fish."

Before it closed in the '80s, Chicago's Don the Beachcomber inspired many imitators, which made the Windy City a center of the tiki craze. There were Kon Tiki Ports (505 North Michigan Avenue), South Pacific Restaurant (28 West Randolph Street) and Shanghai Lil's (5415 North Milwaukee Avenue). Shangri-La (222 North State Street) opened in 1944 in a former movie theater, with a kitchen where the stage had been and a staircase connecting the balcony with the main floor. It advertised itself as the World's Most Romantic Restaurant, but that didn't stop the Internal Revenue Service from closing the place in 1968 for back taxes.

Typically sedate and serious Hyde Park had at least two big tiki restaurants. The Tropical Hut (aka "T-Hut") opened in 1941 on Fifty-Seventh Street near Kenwood Avenue. When urban renewal pushed the restaurant out in 1966, T-Hut moved into a pagoda-like building at Ninety-Second Street and Stony Island Avenue. The place was decorated with bamboo and cabana-like booths covered with "thatch" made of metal strands. Despite the garish décor and so-so food, T-Hut thrived until at least the early '90s.

Also in Hyde Park, Ciral's House of Tiki Lounge (aka "the Tiki") operated at 1612 East Fifty-Third Street from 1962 to 2000, most of the

Don the Beachcomber featured more than eighty kinds of rum and sixty-five original drinks, such as the Missionary's Downfall. *Eric Bronsky.*

time with an after-hours liquor license. Locals remember Tiki Ted and Tiki Bea, who ran the place, as well as the blowfish lamps and the tacky décor. A former Hyde Parker still laughs about a sign in the window that said, "Homemade Jell-O." Others recall the bright neon sign with the restaurant's name and the six-shot Zombie served in a naked-lady glass, even to go. In the 1989 movie *The Package*, House of Tiki provided the location for a scene that showed Gene Hackman frolicking beneath the restaurant's fake palm trees.

Don the Beachcomber's main competitor was Trader Vic's, opened as Traders in 1957 on the lower level of the Palmer House at 17 East Monroe Street. It cost more than $500,000 to create the six-room site that featured massive Maori beams, carved Easter Island heads, totem poles, tribal masks, buoys, canoes and other Polynesian ephemera, all dramatically lit. The restaurant was classy but served the same pseudo Chinese food that was found in other tiki hangouts. Naturally, the drinks, such as the Samoan Fog Cutter and the Suffering Bastard, were strong. The menu listed the Scorpion as a drink that did not "shilly-shally in getting you underway." And these libations were available by the punch bowl!

Trader Vic's threw more than $500,000 into decorating its restaurant in the Palmer House with totem poles, masks, Easter Island heads and more. *Chicago History Museum.*

Like Don the Beachcomber, Trader Vic's was a chain that started in California. Its founder, Vic Bergeron, was inspired by a visit to the original Don the Beachcomber in the mid-'30s. He and Beach would remain rivals, both claiming, for example, to have invented the Mai Tai. Ultimately, Bergeron opened about twenty-five Trader Vic's restaurants nationwide.

Trader Vic's in the Palmer House closed in 2005 but reopened at 1030 North State Street three years later. By then, however, tiki restaurants providing liquid vacations to a different state of mind—"beaches, moonlight and half naked girls," as Bergeron put it—were passé. In 2011, Trader Vic's went to that big Luau in the Sky. But Chicagoans can still don Hawaiian shirts and pursue their island dreams without leaving town. The acclaimed Three Dots and a Dash offers a limited food menu but a seemingly unlimited assortment of enticing cocktails. The Lost Lake tiki bar (3154 West Diversey Avenue), on the border of Logan Square and Polynesia, boasts 275 varieties of rum!

DINING WITH A VIEW

Sky-high dining was not a real possibility in Chicago until the construction of the forty-one-story Prudential Building in 1955. During the previous two decades, which included the Depression and World War II, no skyscrapers were built in Chicago. Then postwar prosperity put the building cranes back to work. The Prudential broke Chicago's building standstill, and its fortieth-floor rooftop restaurant, Stouffer's Top of the Rock, offered spectacular views of downtown, Grant Park and Lake Michigan and provided the world's fastest elevators to get there.

Originally a lounge (where a cocktail cost only one cool dollar), Top of the Rock was converted into a restaurant in 1959 and became the talk of the town—not due to its standard American menu but rather for its stunning panoramic views. One of the restaurant's taglines was "Cocktails in the clouds." Top of the Rock was the place to go for a special occasion or to impress a date, according to the *Tribune*: "Actors, royalty, politicians and athletes all visited during their Chicago visits. Thousands of young couples, arm in arm, dreamed of their lives together while the endless maze of city lights twinkled below."

Despite its elegance, Top of the Rock was not super expensive, perhaps because of competition from newer restaurants in ever taller buildings. When it closed in 1976, the site was converted into a private club with event space.

When Club on 39 opened in 1962 on the, you guessed it, thirty-ninth floor of the United of America Building (1 East Wacker Drive), the *Tribune* called the restaurant "Chicago's newest swankery." It was built around an interior kitchen to maximize the number of tables with window views. The place projected a quiet, dignified look, with paneled wood and bubble chandeliers, all of which won architectural and interior design awards.

Stouffer's Top of the Rock offered spectacular views of Grant Park and the Loop from the fortieth floor of the Prudential Building. *Author's collection.*

Club on 39 catered to men, especially the business lunch crowd. It boasted of "executive men's swivel chairs," and its waitresses wore miniskirts. The club was expensive, with leather menus decorated with white and gold lettering and lasted as a club until at least the mid-'70s, when it was converted to a public restaurant. It continued to provide a bank of plug-in telephones—some of which were imprinted with the names of former club members or distinguished regulars—that could be taken tableside in those pre-cellphone days.

Nearby during the same period, diners could eat at the posh 71 Club in the Executive House (now Wyndham Grand Chicago Riverfront) at 71 East Wacker Drive. Coincidentally, it was also on the thirty-ninth floor. The 71 Club also started as a private club but later opened up to the public, at least for dinner. (Still later, it rechristened itself Seventy-One and, in 1981, Seasons in the Penthouse.)

Food at the 71 Club was "as topflight as the handsomely appointed setting," said one reviewer. It was also known to be quite expensive and exclusive, reflected by the menu that was written entirely in French, as in "escalope de ris de veau, sauce veloutée." Maybe the high prices were needed to pay for the large live trees that adorned the dining room. The restaurant's all-glass walls offered breathtaking views. In fact, the introduction to *The Bob Newhart Show* on television that pictures the impressive lineup of bridges over the Chicago River was filmed from 71 Club's open terrace, where one could dine in good weather.

Café la Tour opened in 1964 and occupied the fortieth floor of the Outer Drive East apartment building (400 East Randolph Street). Floor-to-ceiling windows framed spectacular views of the city, and the surrounding terrace offered outdoor dining. A podium in the main dining room allowed the chef to prepare some dishes in full view of the audience—er, diners.

The South Side also had a rooftop restaurant, albeit not very high. House of Eng on the twelfth floor of the Del Prado Hotel (1701 East Fifty-Third Street) offered striking views of Jackson Park, the Chicago skyline and Lake Michigan. The restaurant, said to be styled after a speakeasy, began in the '40s in the Gold Coast and settled in at the Del Prado in the late '60s. In 1978, the restaurant added a "bubble roof" over its outside seating area.

REVOLVING RESTAURANTS

Other sky-high restaurants took a different spin. Chicago never had something with the stature of the Space Needle, that awesome Seattle landmark with its SkyCity Restaurant revolving five hundred feet above the ground, but it has had at least two revolving rooftop restaurants.

The first was the Carousel in the Sky that opened in 1959 atop the forty-six-story tower of the Morrison Hotel at Clark and Madison Streets. As its name suggests, the restaurant included a working merry-go-round that featured some antique hand-carved carousel horses from Germany's Black Forest. The custom-made carousel, with brass rings, was elevated and set back from the windows, allowing for a row of tables next to the windows. Those on the carousel could eventually see every skyscraper without leaving their saddles.

Previously, the lofty space had been used as a "plush penthouse for the favored few," as one *Tribune* columnist put it. Its transformation into the Carousel in the Sky public restaurant in 1959 included replacing windows with "glass walls" that afforded sweeping views of the city from almost any table. Since the windows were cleaned every other day, "any haziness can be blamed strictly on the weatherman," the columnist added.

The restaurant was used for many charity events and ritzy fashion shows, which made for odd photos in the society pages of fancily dressed women posing on carousel horses. Despite its panoramic views and being appreciated as a romantic setting, Carousel in the Sky lasted until only 1964, perhaps in part due to its unusual, even weird, theme. In any event, the Morrison Hotel was demolished the following year.

Another revolving restaurant, the Pinnacle, opened in 1964 atop the Holiday Inn at 644 North Lake Shore Drive. This led to reports that the Carousel in the Sky's mechanism had been moved there, but this has not been verified. The plush Pinnacle feasted on Chicago history and lore. Its walls were decorated with photos of historic figures, and dishes were named after famous Windy City people, places and things, such as the Union Station (shrimp flambéed with Pernod) and Mattie Silks' Escort (Long Island duckling with Bing cherry sauce named after a notorious madam).

Holiday Inn had a thing for rooftop rotating restaurants, operating several of them around the country, from Baltimore to Des Moines. In any event, Day's Inn purchased the Holiday Inn on Lake Shore Drive and kept the thirty-third-floor Pinnacle restaurant open and spinning, once an hour, until at least the mid-'90s. Currently, the W Chicago Lakeshore Hotel owns the building and rents the former restaurant for private events, but without the spinning turntable.

MAGIC ON THE MENU

Close-up magic (aka bar or tableside magic) was reportedly invented in Chicago, and the Windy City was once the epicenter for such trickery. Recently, however, this restaurant genre has pulled a disappearing act, or nearly so.

The term refers to magic performed at a restaurant bar or table—right before your eyes—rather than on a stage or, even easier to pull off, in an auditorium or on television. The proximity of the table-hopping magicians makes the gags and tricks more awesome because the audience of, say, two to six people think they should be able to spot the close-at-hand sleight of hand. But they can't.

Pick a card, any card. Sign it. Look out…it reappears folded in a matchbook! Or the magician makes coins disappear and oranges appear under seemingly empty cups. Or the magician shuffles the cards, and with a tap, they return to their original order. In your face!

Some of the magicians were veritable comedians, and their quick wit and amusing patter were almost as engaging as their captivating magic tricks. "For close-up magic, you gotta be fast and entertaining," magician Charles Schulien told the *Sun-Times* in 1990.

Above: Although it served a contemporary cuisine, Ivanhoe (3000 North Clark Street), with its castlesque exterior, was patterned after Walter Scott's novel about life in medieval England. *R. V. Mehlenbeck photo. Krambles-Peterson Archive.*

Opposite: Schulien's, seen here in 1985, was famous for table-side tricks and sleight of hand. The magic worked for more than a century. *Robert Krueger photo. Chicago Public Library, Northside Neighborhood History Collection.*

Charles is the son of Matt Schulien, who is credited with conjuring up close-up magic. Matt's father, Joseph, opened a bar in 1881 at LaSalle and Randolph Streets that became a hangout for vaudeville performers. These show people taught Matt a few magic tricks, and he became enthralled with the skill. He even hobnobbed a bit with Harry Houdini. At first Joseph didn't approve, telling Matt to "put the cards away and tend bar." After he realized, however, that his son's tricks would amuse customers and bring in more business, he told his son, "Get out your cards, I'll tend bar." Thus, in the 1910s, close-up restaurant magic was born.

In 1949, the eatery moved to 2100 West Irving Park Road and was renamed Schulien's Restaurant & Saloon. It was a handsome combination of restaurant and tavern with dark woods, stained glass and a long mahogany bar and was decorated with antiques and framed historical photographs.

By all accounts, "Big" Matt, at 320 pounds with a booming radio voice, was quite a guy. During Prohibition, he ran the restaurant as a speakeasy, for which he was reportedly arrested several times. He specialized in rapid-fire magic tricks and sleight of hand, interlaced with one-liners. One gag was to pretend to swallow a live goldfish, but actually Matt used a piece of carrot, sliced beforehand to look like a goldfish.

After Charles retired, Matt's grandson Bob Schulien kept the enterprise going. The acts attracted diminishing returns, however, so in 1999, Schulien's ended its 118-year run. O'Donovan's Pub and Restaurant took over the space and features magic performers on the weekend.

Over the years, tableside tricks became known as Chicago Style Magic and spread beyond Schulien's to enthrall patrons at more than fifteen additional local bars and restaurants, including the Pickle Barrel in Rogers Park; Ivanhoe in Lakeview; Ciao Ristorante in Old Town; Pump Room in the Gold Coast; Little Bit of Magic (a pioneering club at Sixty-First Street and Pulaski Road that also held stage acts until it closed in 1979); and the New York Lounge at 5151 North Lincoln Avenue, where magicians performed tableside seven days a week from 1945 to 1985.

OFFBEAT RESTAURANTS

Chances R (1528 North Wells Street) opened in 1961 and is fondly remembered for burgers, cold beer and a menu shaped like a beer stein—but mostly for the fact that you could throw peanut shells on the hardwood floor. This practice demonstrated that the owners had a sense of humor, as did the name of the restaurant, reportedly derived from the thought, "Chances are we could go broke!" Au contraire. It was so popular that Chances R opened several branches. Known for being integrated, the one at 5225 South Harper Avenue appealed equally to South Siders and members of the University of Chicago.

Chances R on Wells Street was part of the emergence of Old Town in the '60s as a counterculture district. Run-down storefronts were being transformed into hippie hangouts, headshops, folk music venues, art galleries and comedy clubs. Old Town also attracted many unique eateries, including the original Moody's Pub (in 1959 at 1529 North Wells Street, but it's successor still serves beer and burgers at 5910 North Broadway) and the Fireplace Inn (opened in 1968 at 1448 North Wells Street and still going strong, known for barbecue ribs and a dark, romantic atmosphere).

The Pickle Barrel, another memorable restaurant in raucous Old Town, opened in 1960 at 1423 North Wells Street. A barrel of dill pickles greeted you when you walked in, and its walls were covered with oddities. There were free pickles and popcorn at every table, presumably to outdo the free peanuts at Chances R. "During an average week, the restaurant would go through 10 barrels of pickles and 400 pounds of popcorn," said Chicago historian and WTTW program host extraordinaire Geoffrey Baer. "Balloon artists entertained the kids, and pitchers of beer entertained the adults."

The Pickle Barrel was known for its Sunday "blunch," served a bit later in the day than brunch. This featured an all-you-can-eat affair from a well-loaded buffet called a "smeargasbord," so called because the butter spread smoothly on your toast, as did the cream cheese on your bagel. So many people came that a rope had to be strung up along the sidewalk to keep customers in line. Such success led to four more Pickle Barrels, including one at 50 East Oak Street and another at Howard Street and Western Avenue. But the times, they kept a changin'. The last Pickle Barrel restaurant closed in 1983.

Sometime in the late '70s, the peanut shells at the original Chances R in Old Town were swept up for the last time. A sign for the Sir Loin Inn was hung out front, but only for a fictional restaurant in a scene in the movie *The Color of Money*. "Loin" might have referred to the adult bookstores that peppered Wells Street, but today, Old Town is squeaky clean, even upscale.

In a meat-and-potatoes town, vegetarian restaurants have also been considered offbeat. There were many, but none ever hit the big time. Chicago is not San Francisco or Ann Arbor, Michigan. The avant-garde Voltaire (3231 North Clark Street) was better known for is alternative performance space in the basement than for its vegetarian fare on the ground floor. Nearby, the Bread Shop Kitchen (3411 North Halsted Street, across the street from its wonderful namesake cooperative health food store and bakery) made a mission of serving wholesome vegetarian food in a groovy setting during the '70s. Today, the Chicago Diner continues that healthy tradition in the same location.

THE SCOOP ON ICE CREAM PARLORS

Ice cream has long been served in Chicago, starting as early as 1844 at the city's first free-standing restaurant, the Exchange Coffee House on Clark Street. An ad from 1853 told of J.P. Heth's Soda Water and Ice Cream

Saloon at 163 North Randolph Street for "the reception of those who wish to imbibe the luxuries and delicacies the season affords."

Many ice cream "saloons" were aimed at women, who early in the city's history were not welcome in male-dominated saloons and taverns or unaccompanied in legitimate restaurants. But in the 1880s, women could frequent Gunther's spectacular candy factory and café on State Street for light meals, coffee and ice cream. On the floor above the café, founder Charles Gunther displayed priceless historic artifacts he had collected around the country, including the bed in which Abraham Lincoln died, which is now on exhibit at the Chicago History Museum. (Chicagoans must have been eating a lot of candy and ice cream, as Gunther could afford in 1889 to purchase the Confederate Libby Prison in Richmond, Virginia, and have it transported to Chicago and reconstructed at 1500 South Wabash Avenue as the third Chicago Coliseum.)

Buffalo Ruled the Scene for Decades

The original Buffalo Ice Cream Parlor was opened in 1908 at Division and Sedgwick Streets and named after Buffalo, New York, the hometown of the original owner. Between 1918 and 1920, Greek immigrants John and Mike Korompilas moved Buffalo to a spacious, highly visible store at the northwest corner of Irving Park and Crawford (now Pulaski) Roads. They kept much of the elaborate décor, which featured stained-glass windows; wood booths with narrow, black glass–topped tables; a marble-topped soda fountain bar; and vintage cherub murals. Buffalo became a popular spot for families, after-schoolers and dates.

The Korompilases sold the parlor in 1943 because they were having difficulty finding enough workers during World War II, but new owners were able to keep the soda-and-sundae palace going. Oddly by today's standards, Buffalo served only vanilla, chocolate and strawberry ice cream. It was made off-site to the store's recipe, but the toppings were made in-house. In 1973, the property owners announced plans to demolish the building that housed Buffalo and replace it with a Shell gas station. A group of sweet-tooth activists forestalled that plan, but eventually in 1978, Buffalo got stampeded by the gas station. The ice cream parlor moved to 1180 West Lake Cook Road in Buffalo Grove, where it still scoops out cones and shakes, as well as a full menu of contemporary American food. Photos of the former restaurant decorate the walls.

Zephyr, seen here in 1985, was one of many shops that scooped up delicious ice cream treats. Other notables include Doctor Jazz, Buffalo and Gertie's. *Robert Krueger photo. Chicago Public Library, Northside Neighborhood History Collection.*

All that Jazz

Many other Chicago ice cream palaces have similarly melted away. Doctor Jazz Ice Cream Parlor (1609 West Montrose Avenue), for example, opened in 1970 and closed after about seventeen years. It was famous for its thick peanut butter shakes, created from homemade ice cream. The loud, zany place was also exceptional for several restored nickelodeons, a working player piano and antique amusement games rescued from Riverview Park. As if to balance the cacophony, silent movies played regularly. Occasionally, a Charlie Chaplin impersonator greeted customers. (A second Doctor Jazz operated for a time on Chicago Avenue in Evanston.)

In the days before restaurants introduced nonsmoking sections, Doctor Jazz pioneered the idea that smoking should not be tolerated in restaurants. And it had a novel way of enforcing the rule: If a customer lit up, smoke detectors would set off sirens and fans. This pioneering stance encouraged this author in the '70s to attend meetings of Chicago's Alliance of Non-Smokers at Doctor Jazz. Once, the young bow tie–wearing Forty-Third Ward alderman Martin Oberman met with alliance members at the ice cream parlor to talk about his support for a citywide no-smoking ordinance aimed at restaurants. "Smoking is not only obnoxious; it's also a very serious health problem," he said. At the time, that was a radical statement, and that day was a heady one for the ragtag group of young activists.

Doctor Jazz was so recognized for supporting the rights of nonsmokers to breathe clean air that in 1975, the American Cancer Society gave it an award—its first ever to a restaurant for helping to fight cancer. Doctor Jazz closed in 1986 or 1987.

The owners of Doctor Jazz, Mike and Joe Bortz, ran another unconventional entertainment emporium called Sally's Stage (6345 North Western Avenue). In 1977, they bought the building that had previously housed Sally's Original Bar-B-Q. Reportedly, they didn't like the name "Sally's," but they did like the big recognizable sign out front that bore that word. In the end, they added the word "Stage" to the bright red sign and settled on "Sally's Stage" as the name of their restaurant.

This wacky restaurant featured roller-skating waitresses who delivered food to the customers along a roller rink that passed by the tables. Along the way, they would sing—with or without accompaniment by the restaurant's huge theatrical pipe organ, snare drum and other percussion. Customers would sing along or even jump up onstage and perform. Off-the-wall entertainment include Men's Leg Night, Western Night and a children's rodeo. Magicians, clowns, belly dancers and other eclectic performers would also regale customers.

This cavernous cathedral of convoluted taste was a popular destination for kid's birthday parties, well before Chuck E. Cheese sold its first token in Chicago. The Bortz brothers sold Sally's Stage in 1983, and the new owners kept the same song and dance going for at least a couple more years.

Gertie's Ice Cream Parlor, a beloved dessert hangout, opened in 1901 at Fifty-Ninth Street and Kedzie Avenue. This treasured eatery, once featured in an episode of *Crime Story*, is long gone, but Gertie's ice cream is still available at Lindy's Chili (a chain that started in 1924 and now operates a few local restaurants).

The Original Rainbow Cone, opened in 1926 at 9233 South Western Avenue, closes during the winter but otherwise keeps scooping out ice cream at its historic original location. Gone, however, is Farrell's Ice Cream Parlour

& Restaurant, a loud, old-fashioned place where they used to beat a big drum to celebrate someone's birthday. The beloved Zephyr Ice Cream Restaurant (1777 West Wilson Avenue) sported a distinctive streamlined, Art Deco interior with mirrored walls. It served scandalously huge concoctions such as a sixty-four-ounce "Marathon Milkshake" and a ten-scoop "War of the Worlds" sundae. Truly something to scream about, Zephyr opened in the mid-'70s and closed in 2006.

Margie's Candies (1960 North Western Avenue) opened in 1921 and is still serving ice cream sundaes, splits and shakes, as well as homemade candies. It offers a wonderful sense of what some of the old, attractive, ever-so-tempting ice cream parlors and candy concerns were like—and what Chicago has lost as these treasures have disappeared, leaving the city, in the eyes of some, a veritable dessert desert.

SPORTS

Innumerable sports-themed restaurants have come and gone in the Windy City, a true sports mecca. A relatively early one, Johnny Lattner's Steak House (105 West Madison Street), opened in 1962. A longtime Oak Park resident, Lattner played football at Notre Dame, winning the Heisman Trophy in 1953, which landed him on the cover of *Time* magazine. After a fire destroyed his restaurant in 1968, he rebuilt in Marina City in the space now occupied by Dick's Last Resort. Johnny Lattner's Marina City operated until 1973.

Few people remember Lattner or his steakhouse, but most local and many out-of-towners recollect Michael Jordan's Restaurant at 500 North LaSalle Street, opened in 1993. Its most remarkable feature was the twenty-five-foot-diameter cutout Wilson basketball on the roof of the building that could be seen from many blocks away. The sign—now plain white—still sits atop the building. It should be decorated as a giant-sized pizza, as Gino's East now occupies the building.

The first floor of Michael Jordan's housed a sports bar with in-your-face television screens all around. The bar and restaurant was packed during Chicago Bulls games. The first floor also sported a gift shop for the hordes of tourists who flocked to this holy ground, hoping to catch a glimpse of Jordan, who was rumored to frequent the place, although most often in his private dining room. The second floor housed the main two-hundred-seat dining room.

Michael Jordan's was located at 500 North La Salle Street in an 1888 building that was built as a cable car powerhouse to drive underground cables. *Chicago History Museum.*

The restaurant went a bit overboard in acclaiming the admittedly considerable accomplishments of number 23. The front of the restaurant was dominated by a gaudy thirty- by thirty-foot vinyl banner of Jordan floating overhead. In case you missed that, a large portrait of His Airness hung just inside, where patrons could also find innumerable photos, jerseys, trophies and shoes. The food was generally regarded as mediocre.

In 1999, as Jordan pulled out due to slipping sales, rumor had it that Chicago Cubs baseball star Sammy Sosa would take over the space, but that never materialized. Soon thereafter, Jordan opened a new restaurant at 505 North Michigan Avenue that prides itself on the "steaksmanship" of dry-aged beef.

The handsome red brick 500 North LaSalle Street building has a remarkable history. Charles Tyson Yerkes, Chicago's colorful transit titan, built the three-story structure in 1888 as a cable car powerhouse. It housed enormous stationary engines that drove cables, some of them three miles long, under LaSalle Street, the Chicago River and streets of the Loop to pull cable cars along their routes. In 1929, when LaSalle Street was widened, the façade of the building was moved back seventeen feet. Workers faithfully re-created the front, so the building is largely intact, something that helped it earn Chicago Landmark status in 2001.

Over the years, the building housed other eateries, including Lalo's Mexican Restaurant. Its longest-lasting and most interesting food tenant was Ireland's, at one time the country's largest exclusive seafood restaurant.

Da Bears

The Chicago Bears generated a few restaurants over the years as their fortunes flew and fell. One of the most visible was Ditka's Restaurant (223 West Ontario Street) and the adjoining City Lights nightclub, opened in 1986 while "Iron" Mike Ditka was still coaching the Bears. This surprised many people who thought it would distract the coach and team that had just won the Super Bowl.

Ditka was one of the most recognizable sports figures in the country, and his steaks and chops restaurant did well, even becoming one of the highest-grossing eateries in the country. Diners rubbed shoulders with many sports celebrities, and the two adjoining places featured mystery nights, electronic ticker tapes with the latest sports results and the Skyliner dance troupe composed of the restaurant's wait staff. The food, such as the Fullback-Size Filet Mignon and Da Pork Chop, was good, too. But the high-rent district restaurant fell short and closed in 1992, apparently blitzed by debt, surrounded by controversy, bruised by bad publicity and sacked by legal and management issues. The following year, the Bears fired Ditka, but "Da Coach" now runs a chain of restaurants called Ditka's, including a location at 100 East Chestnut Street that is especially popular with tourists.

Several other Bears tried their hand in the food service industry, and many of them found that catching passes in midair or barreling through linebackers was easier than running a restaurant. Jim McMahon, quarterback of that 1986 Super Bowl team, struggled with his own restaurant, which he opened in 1987 at Lincoln and Armitage Avenues in what had been a popular Mexican restaurant called Hacienda del Sol. It served basic, straight-up American food.

Jim McMahon's Restaurant lasted only two years, in part because McMahon was not "Mac the Nice" with the press, which alienated the media. The downstairs space was labeled "Jim McMahon's Press Club—No Press Allowed." The restaurant "was opened with all the brashness of a cocky quarterback, but it seemed to close like a losing team slinking out of town on the last bus—at night, unannounced, with only a few passersby looking on," is how *Sun-Times* columnist Neil Steinberg described the situation in 1989.

McMahon later told the press he closed the restaurant since he wasn't making any money from it, even though it seemed packed most of the time. Also, it made too many demands on his personal life. "I was always getting told that I had to be there all the time," McMahon told the *Tribune* in 2002. "But I told them, 'I have a family. My wife can cook.'"

While it lasted (2010–17), Jimmy Green's was a popular sports-oriented restaurant. Located at 825 South State Street close to Soldier Field, the typically loud bar with television screens everywhere was probably counting on great support from Bears fans. Alas, Jimmy Green's timing was off because the Monsters of the Midway were pathetic many of the years the restaurant was open, something that must have contributed to the restaurant's early demise.

Overall, Chicago's sports-oriented restaurants have not been especially memorable or distinctive. Most of them served bar food, had too many loud televisions and lasted only as long as the fleeting fame of their namesakes. There are exceptions, of course, such as Harry Caray's Italian Steakhouse, named after the legendary sports broadcaster. It was open in 1987 and is still going strong. Holy cow, indeed!

CHAPTER 11

Delis, Diners and Dogs

Chicago has seen hundreds of deli-cious delis come and go—from Moe's to Max's to Minnie's. These eateries are remembered for any number of reasons. At Braverman's, "the corned beef really came thru the rye," as its slogan said. And to enter Silverstein's, customers would sometimes have to work through a crowd of soapbox orators and hecklers.

For most of the twentieth century, hundreds of neighborhood delis served up affordable sandwiches and salads, while dozens of traditional delis dotted the Loop, where shoppers were never far from a thick pastrami sandwich, half-sour pickle and generous serving of homemade soup. Sadly, these delis have by and large disappeared, driven out by the high cost of meat and the proliferation of sandwich and fast-food chain stores.

NATE'S

One of Chicago's oldest delicatessens was Nate's Deli (807 West Maxwell Street). Its origins go back to 1908 as Lyon's Grocery, and in 1924, it moved to Maxwell Street and opened as a restaurant. The small place offered a rare comfort on Maxwell Street: a place to sit down. It became known for traditional Jewish food, such as kosher-style corned beef and pickled herring. Employee Nate Duncan bought the deli in 1972 and renamed it for himself. An African American, Nate continued the Jewish menu and learned kosher-style cooking from the former owner's mother. He even learned to speak Yiddish.

Nate's hit the big time thanks to scenes in the 1980 movie *The Blues Brothers*, in which legendary John Lee Hooker plays the blues outside the restaurant and superstar Aretha Franklin sings the female anthem "Think" inside the cramped restaurant. Despite such fame, this Chicago icon closed in 1995 shortly before the building it occupied was razed to make room for expansion of the University of Illinois at Chicago—and, some say, as part of university and city efforts to "sanitize" Maxwell Street. A *Sun-Times* editorial lamenting the loss of Nate's called the deli the "soul of Maxwell Street" and said, "Neither global competition nor crime nor national franchises killed Nate's. It was killed by the lack of imagination of a public university and the lack of sensitivity of city politicians."

ASHKENAZ

What probably became Chicago's most beloved deli was started in the 1910s on the West Side by George and Ida Ashkenaz. In 1940, they followed members of the Jewish immigrant community to East Rogers Park, opening up shop at 1432 West Morse Avenue. It became renowned for its extensive menu, with more than 350 items. The soups, the salads! The sandwiches, the pastries! Virtually all of it homemade. Over the years, Ashkenaz reportedly grew into Chicago's largest Jewish deli, serving more than half a ton of corned beef per month (to which someone quipped, "Yes, but that would make only five sandwiches at Ashkenaz!").

Beth Montcalm Campe, who waitressed at Ashkenaz, credits the enjoyable experience with awakening her *goy* palate. "It was the first time I tasted kreplach, kishke, cabbage soup, gefilte fish and more. I still love a good bowl of matzo ball soup." Campe also remembers a wonderful sense of community among both the staff and customers there. "You felt neighborliness toward everyone, whether they lived in Rogers Park or had driven in from Highland Park or Hyde Park," she said.

Ashkenaz became a landmark. "Anyone who knows a bagel from a blintz…knew about Ashkenaz," said the *Tribune* in 1976. Alas, the restaurant closed that year. Another owner took over the space and renamed it Ashkey's. Meanwhile, Ashkenaz shifted gears, opening completely different renditions of itself on the North Shore and at 14 East Cedar Street (in 1990), the latter a carryout storefront, but now closed.

The legendary Ashkenaz, seen here from the "L" platform, was located in Rogers Park but attracted customers from far and wide. *Rogers Park/West Ridge Historical Society.*

MORT'S DELI

Mort Steinberg got his start in the business working at the legendary Ashkenaz delicatessen. Later, he opened his own place on the North Side and then opened a deli downtown on Dearborn Street. It was so popular that he opened another one across the street. In 1980, Steinberg opened Mort's Deli at 159 North Wabash Avenue, which morphed into one of Chicago's best-known delis. The food was great, but Mort himself was the main attraction. Customers described him as caring and well connected. He fed homeless people. He taught protégés how to cook and gave them a place to stay. He even loaned friends his Thunderbird. And for years, Mort's gave a free cup of soup to customers in the winter and slice of watermelon in the summer.

Mort's Deli under the "L" typified downtown delis that served sandwiches stacked high with corned beef. It was beloved by tourists and locals alike. *University of Illinois at Chicago Library.*

Although Steinberg was brusque with some customers, he had a sense of humor. His restaurant sat under the noisy Loop "L," and a sign there described the place as "'L'egant dining under the cars." Mort's was anything but elegant, with its crowded seating, plastic plants and teeming traffic out front. Yet Steinberg was one of the first downtown restaurants to install a sidewalk café after the City of Chicago finally permitted this polished Parisian practice in 1985. The deli closed in 1993.

The heavyset, ever-present Steinberg "was a true Chicago character," Governor Jim Thompson said after the restaurateur died in 2010. "In the era of mass market consumer outlets, I miss the personal, gruff caring of guys like Mort."

OTHER DELIS

The Bagel Restaurant opened in 1950 at 4806 North Kedzie Avenue as a tiny restaurant with only six tables and ten counter stools. There were often lines out the door of this family-run deli, not only because it had limited seating but also because the food was so good, mostly homemade. In 1977, it moved to larger quarters at 3000 West Devon Avenue, where it thrived. It was one of the more attractive Jewish sit-down restaurants in Chicago. As one *Tribune* critic said in 1981 about The Bagel's décor, "This type of cuisine doesn't often come with ambiance, unless you're turned on by taking a number." In addition, the warm, welcoming restaurant offered a wide variety of Jewish food, far beyond bagels and lox, "specialties that even your grandmother may have forgotten," the paper said, such as grilled kippered herring with fried onions, matzo brie, smoked sablefish and schmaltz herring. In 1992, The Bagel moved to 3107 North Broadway, where it still does a bustling business.

Likewise, Mama Batt's Restaurant offered authentic home cooking. Regular customers knew better than to ask for a recipe. "If you want one,

The Bagel was a deli with a full-service restaurant that served Jewish specialties, even some "your grandmother may have forgotten." *Robert Krueger photo. Chicago Public Library, Northside Neighborhood History Collection.*

come at 5 a.m. and watch," co-owner Nate Batt told the *Tribune* in 1975. The delicatessen opened in 1921 on the West Side and moved a few times, ending up in 1956 at 112 East Cermak Road on the ground floor of the New Michigan Hotel, also known as the Lexington Hotel. Al Capone was said to use this hotel as his Chicago headquarters. "We had a lot of gangsters come down here," co-owner Sam Batt told the *Tribune*. "They'd sit in a booth and spend the time making deals as though this was their office—except we were paying the rent."

Despite such nefarious activity, customers kept coming back to Batt's, not only for the sweet and sour cabbage and other Jewish treats but also for the restaurant's two-hundred-car parking lot on Cermak Road. Batt's provided diners with free parking and, from there, shuttle service to McCormick Place and nearby sports venues. It closed in 1980.

Bob Elfman's Sandwich Shop (179 North State Street) opened in 1933, grew into a chain and closed in 1985, but not until it served an estimated 6.76 million pounds of corned beef, give or take a few ounces. This Loop landmark was popular with movie- and theatergoers, as well as the downtown lunch crowd. But the malling of State Street in 1979 and the rise of fast food spelled Elfman's demise. It sold great sandwiches, but it's also remembered for the wall-size vintage photographs of Wrigley Field.

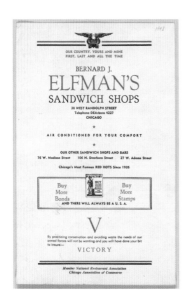

This Elfman's menu cover from 1943 shows patriotic fervor: "By avoiding waste…you will have done your bit to insure victory." *Chicago History Museum.*

The Belden Deli (2315 North Clark Street) was a neighborhood temple of nosh. Locals and theatergoers especially appreciated the restaurant's relaxed, informal atmosphere; ample seating; large portions; and acerbic waitresses. Perhaps most of all, they appreciated the restaurant staying open late, at one time until 1:00 a.m. on weekends and, at other times, twenty-four hours a day. The popular deli opened in 1957 and grew into a chain with four locations. The original restaurant on Clark Street went out on a high note in 1988 or 1989 to make room for the construction of a shopping center.

Eli's Stage Delicatessen (50 East Oak Street) opened in 1958. It developed into a

Left: Eli's Stage Delicatessen (50 East Oak Street) developed into a hangout for Gold Coast residents and a magnet for celebrities. *Marc Schulman.*

Below: Joe Ross—a patrolman in the TV show *Car 54, Where Are You?*—poses with Eli Schulman's son, Marc, at the Stage Deli. *Marc Schulman.*

hangout for Gold Coast residents and a magnet for celebrities, including Barbra Streisand, Joan Rivers, Woody Allen and Sammy Davis Jr., many of whom were performing at Mr. Kelly's (1953–75), a renowned nightclub (which also served food) nearby on Rush Street. The Stage Deli closed in 1968.

You couldn't beat the food or the price at What's Cooking Restaurant and Delicatessen (6107 North Lincoln Avenue). A bowl of hearty soup, together with the free relish plate and the copious amount and variety of fresh breads, would make an entire meal.

D.B. KAPLAN'S

In the '70s, Don Burton Kaplan opened Hemingway's Moveable Feast at 1825 North Lincoln Avenue. It was a first-class place, known for skyscraper sandwiches with outrageous names. He sold it in 1976 to focus on his eponymous deli in the new Water Tower Place, a vertical shopping center at 845 North Michigan Avenue. But the deli's seventh-floor location didn't help business.

In 1978, Larry and Mark Levy invested in D.B. Kaplan's, although they wondered whether many customers would find their way to the top floor of the shopping center. When it became clear that the restaurant was faltering, the Levys brought in a higher power—their mom. The turnaround was almost immediate, as Eadie Levy not only introduced delicious family recipes of Jewish dishes but also helped in the front, welcoming and seating customers and remembering returning ones. Little by little, she became known citywide and eventually served as the face of the Levys' booming restaurant business. "She was like our Colonel Sanders," Larry told the *Chicago Business Journal* in 2017.

D.B. Kaplan's was a friendly, funky place. Its creative menu always provided plenty of laughs, such as stating, "Never before has a delicatessen risen to such great heights (the 7th floor of Water Tower Place)." And it

This 1989 Kaplan's menu cover caricaturizes sports broadcaster Harry Caray, Eadie Levy (the owners' mom) and radio host Robert Murphy. *Eric Bronsky.*

listed a wild assortment of sandwiches, such as the Studs Turkey, Fowl Play, Tongue Fu and the Topless Hugh Hefner Club Sandwich.

The Levys closed D.B. Kaplan's in 1995, by which time the rent in the successful shopping center had skyrocketed. In the meantime, they had opened a similar Mrs. Levy's Deli in the Sears Tower, and that place operated from 1986 to 2006. Eventually, Levy Restaurants reoriented its business toward providing food at sports and entertainment venues. Today, the company does hundreds of millions of dollars of business at some two hundred venues and employs thousands of workers—all growing out of one struggling deli.

DINERS RIDE THE RAILS

Chicago had so many diners that it would take a separate book to do them all justice. Its best-known diner, complete with neon signs, aluminum trim, vinyl booths and jukeboxes, was an ersatz one. The retro Ed Debevic's (640 North Wells Street) opened in 1984 and featured mediocre and relatively expensive food but a lively, entertaining atmosphere. The smart-aleck servers would make snarky remarks, sit at your table to take your order and sometimes even dance on the soda counter.

A couple of the humorous signs that decorated the restaurant said, "Eat at Ed's because you can't bowl there," but "eat and get out." Another sign said, "Children left unattended will be towed at owner's expense." Over the mirror in the men's restroom it said, "This is why you're going home alone tonight." This fun place was mostly frequented by tourists—no surprise given its River North location, near Planet Hollywood (1993–99), a kitschy tourist destination.

Another modern-day diner, Salt & Pepper (2575 North Lincoln Avenue), opened in 1965. The spacious restaurant, with a long counter and plenty of tables, served traditional diner food at affordable prices, fitting for the neighborhood it served, which included DePaul University. Salt & Pepper did especially well while *Million Dollar Quartet* played (3,053 times!) across the street at the Apollo Theater. That popular show told the story of a 1956 recording session that featured Johnny Cash, Jerry Lee Lewis, Carl Perkins and Elvis Presley playing together.

Salt & Pepper expanded with a second outlet in Wrigleyville but closed in 2012. It will be fondly remembered as the site of a bit by standup comedian

John Mulaney in which he put seven dollars in the jukebox for twenty-one consecutive plays of "What's New Pussycat."

Chicago's longest-running diner was probably the beloved Diner Grill (1635 West Irving Park Road), open from 1939 until it succumbed to a fire on Christmas Eve 2016. That's seventy-seven years, a long time for two small abandoned transit cars—thought to be former Evanston Railway streetcars—placed side by side to be serving up bacon and eggs. But the modest place had a loyal following.

The Diner Grill was best known for its "Slinger," consisting of two hamburger patties, two sunny-side up eggs, cheese and hash browns, all smothered with chili, and served with a side of toast. Yes, that's a lot, so anyone who finished it would receive a "Certificate of Completion." The food and experience kept customers coming back to the tiny dive—open 24/7, every day except Christmas. Many of the regulars were in the restaurant industry, looking for a place to eat after a late-night shift. Other late-night patrons, looking for a place to sober up after the bars closed, would trade one bar stool for another and order coffee and comfort food.

In mid-2018, the Diner Grill surprised many by recovering from the fire damage, rising like the legendary Phoenix and reopening. It may last another seventy-seven years.

Being such a train town, it's no surprise that Chicago sported several other diners in converted railroad cars. These cars (dining cars, railroad coaches and transit cars) ended their careers as restaurants because they were cheap to convert and offered a nostalgic "trip" without having to leave town.

Carrying the railroad theme a step further, a restaurant named Track One sat on Track One at the LaSalle Street railroad station near Congress Parkway from which Metra operates today. It consisted of a club car (Pacific Shore) and dining car (Golden Harvest), both rescued from the Golden State Limited service between Chicago and Los Angeles provided by the Chicago, Rock Island & Pacific Railroad, known as "a mighty fine line." And Track One offered some mighty fine dining. To be authentic, experienced trainmen cooked the food in the train's kitchen, cramped as it was. The club car offered drinks and snacks and seated thirty-two, while the dining car seated forty for full meals. Track One opened in 1972 and hit the end of the line only three years later, when the cars were hauled away to an uncertain future.

Perhaps Track One shot too high. Most train cars given a new lease on life as eateries were transformed into short-order diners rather than first-class restaurants. Burlington Diner, one of the former category, was decommissioned as a dining car of unknown origin in 1939 and moved to 4183 South Halsted Street as a restaurant. Locals referred to it as a "pop art" diner because each of the windows contained a different-colored glass. "The effect inside is, to put it mildly, wild," said the *Tribune*.

Based on its location across the street from the Union Stock Yards, the Burlington Diner was probably patronized by visitors to and workers at the stockyards. Also, it stood just a block north of the International Amphitheatre, with a capacity of nine thousand people, so the diner must have been busy during the five national political conventions and innumerable sporting events and concerts held there.

Frank Nadell took a different approach when he spent $100,000 rehabilitating the 40-by-130-foot brick Grand Trunk Western Railroad Station that had been vacant and vandalized over the previous forty years. He opened the Train Station Restaurant (3601 West Sixty-Third Street) in 1973, converting the station into a railroad buff's dream come true. "In this day, with everybody in the food industry coming up with gimmicks, I figured

Burlington Diner at 4183 South Halsted Street was well located near the International Amphitheatre and the Union Stock Yard. *Author's collection.*

a train station was just the ticket," Nadell told the *Tribune*. It's not known whether the restaurant was well patronized or how long it stayed open.

Meanwhile, the Zephyr Diner (Fourteenth and Canal Streets) merely simulated a railroad car. Made of bricks and mortar and about the size of a passenger car, this diner was demolished in the '80s.

At least a couple of old railroad car conversions are still serving good food, along with healthy portions of railroad nostalgia. Since 2002, a 1947 Budd Company car that ran on the Atlantic Coast Line Railroad has sat on a specially built track—with a railroad crossing signal, to boot—at the Silver Palm (768 North Milwaukee Avenue). All meals are cooked in the tiny 220-square-foot kitchen.

And since 1993, Tutto Italiano (501 South Wells Street) has been serving exquisite meals from an old Milwaukee Road dining car. The busy traffic whizzing by on Congress Parkway often gives diners the impression of moving along the railroad. The car is all original—except for the interior windows, which have been replaced with lithographs of train stops in the Chicago area.

These diners and old train cars no longer rock and roll, but they provide a trip down memory lane for rail fans, history buffs and food connoisseurs.

DOGS

Hot dogs are as essential to the Chicago food experience as juicy steaks or deep-dish pizza. Chicago reportedly sports more hot dog vendors than all the McDonald's, Burger King and Wendy's outlets combined.

True, the idea of putting a sausage in a bun that could be eaten quickly and easily, even on the run, is credited to Nathan's on Coney Island in 1916. But Chicago has elevated the hot dog to a higher level, so much higher that the hot dog is now part of the city's indelible identity. Chicagoans insist that there's only one correct way to eat it—"the way nature intended," as columnist Mike Royko once put it: an all-beef frank on a white poppy-seed bun, with yellow mustard, sweet green pickle relish, chopped white onions, four tomato wedges, one dill pickle spear, two sport peppers and a dash of celery salt—in that order! It goes without saying that no ketchup is allowed.

Abe "Fluky" Drexler claimed to have created this formula at Fluky's, a humble portable hot dog stand based near Maxwell Street and Roosevelt Road that he opened in 1929. The catchy name referred to a cruel

Many Chicago diners were in former railroad cars—or even buses, as was the case with the Beulah Eat Shoppe in the 400 block of East Thirty-First Street. *Author's collection.*

childhood prank that Drexler survived. As part of a grade-school initiation, he was dragged up many stairs by a rope tied around his neck. One of the perpetrators later said it was a "fluke" that Drexler didn't die, and the name stuck.

After wheeling around Chicago for thirty-five years, Fluky's opened its first permanent restaurant at the southwest corner of Pratt and Western Avenues in 1964. It prospered, and several additional restaurants followed in the city and suburbs. In 1968, the company opened its flagship, glass-encased store at 6821 North Western Avenue. Competition intensified, however, turning the tide for Fluky's. Its restaurants began closing, and in 2006, U Lucky Dawg purchased Fluky's flagship store. After six years, this restaurant also closed. (That said, one Fluky's remains in the Walmart at 5630 Touhy Avenue in Niles.)

Hot Doug's

Chicago's most beloved hot dog restaurant was Hot Doug's. This Sausage Superstore opened in 2001 at 2314 West Roscoe Street and later moved to 3324 North California Avenue. It woke up the palate of the entire city, serving custom-made sausages of kangaroo, alligator, rattlesnake, wild boar, yak, foie gras and other delicacies. Although the City of Chicago banned foie gras in 2006, Hot Doug's kept serving it, even creating the "Joe Moore" hot dog, named after the alderman who proposed the ban. For serving foie gras, Hot Doug's was fined $250, but owner Doug Sohn later held a "détente" meeting with Moore. The entire controversy generated a lot of good publicity for the restaurant.

Hot Doug's was Chicago most successful hot dog—er, make that encased meats— restaurant. *Doug Sohn.*

Other celebrities honored with hot dogs named after them included Britney Spears, Howard Devoto (co-founder of the Buzzcocks), Larry Potash (a WGN-TV news anchor) and Patricia Adamatis (an Illinois Teacher of the Year).

Popular menu items included duck fat fries and Game of the Week (as in elk, antelope, etc.). And the cheery restaurant featured many creative touches, such as bright primary colors, custom-painted murals, wiener signs, an eclectic playlist and a wall of fame. Folks loved the place, with many loyal customers returning again and again, despite waits as long as several hours.

One day in 2014, Sohn announced he would close his Sausage Superstore in five months. He had decided "it was time to do something else." On the last day, the line was so long that additional customers were turned away at 6:30 a.m.—four hours before the restaurant even opened.

Felony Franks

One place that deserves to be in the Vienna Beef Hot Dog Hall of Fame (yes, there is such a thing) but has been overlooked, perhaps because it was controversial, is Felony Franks. Opened in 2009 at 229 North Western Avenue, this remarkable fast-food eatery was devoted to hiring ex-offenders. It made the most of this idea by promoting rather than hiding its mission. Its logo featured a hot dog in prison garb, and one of its advertisements read, "Food so good it's criminal." Meanwhile, its menu was packed with such items as the Misdemeanor Wiener, Breakout Burger and Parolish (a Polish sausage sandwich). A portion of Felony Franks profits went to Rescue Foundation, a nonprofit that helped ex-offenders.

This openness must have raised the ire of its neighbors, who went to their alderman, Bob Fioretti, to oppose Felony Franks. The Second Ward alderman objected to the name and blocked the restaurant's application for a permit to put up a sign with the restaurant's logo. The permit was finally approved in 2011, but not until the City of Chicago had racked up $800,000 in legal fees alone. Besides, by then the restaurant was going under due to a lack of business.

In 2014, Felony Franks reopened in the more open-minded town of Oak Park, where it set up shop, sign and all, at 6427 West North Avenue. "People who live in Oak Park see the rehabilitation and help of ex-offenders as a good thing…and are very excited," Deno Andrews, the son of the restaurant's founder, told the newspaper.

Not excited enough, apparently. Felony Franks closed for good in 2017. Dog gone it!

Today, for a true Chicago hot dog in an old-time classic setting, check out Byron's, a family-owned hot dog group with locations at 1701 West Lawrence Avenue and 1017 West Irving Park Road. Along with Hot Doug's, Wiener Circle, Wolfy's, Gold Coast Dogs, Skyway Dogs and many others, Byron's is in the Hot Dog Hall of Fame.

CHAPTER 12

Movers and Shakers

ELI SCHULMAN (1910–1988)

Eli Schulman was a successful restaurateur and also one of Chicago's most recognized and influential personalities of his day. He ran several restaurants but also worked in public service: as a ward precinct captain for twenty-five years, a job he compared with social work; as deputy city coroner for four years; and as a commissioner of the North Shore mosquito abatement district. He knew politics, counted mayors and movie stars among his friends and was a major philanthropist. A plaque at the Eli Schulman Playground in Seneca Park reads, "Eli embodies the determination, the open-armed spirit and the street-smart charm of the city he loved."

Schulman began his restaurant career in 1940 with Eli's Ogden Huddle, a coffeehouse at 3201 West Ogden Avenue. Here he made news by putting a sign in the window that said, "If you are hungry and have no money, come in. We will feed you." Next up was his successful Eli's Stage Delicatessen at 50 East Oak Street, open from 1958 until 1968. There, Schulman handed out advice and extended friendship with the sandwiches.

All the while, Schulman wanted a white-tablecloth restaurant. Finally, he opened Eli's The Place for Steak at 215 East Chicago Avenue in 1966. The glitzy restaurant became a mecca for who's who in Chicago, and Schulman always liked to be there to greet them, have a photo taken with them and introduce them to family members. Schulman worked six days a week until

The ever-gregarious Eli Schulman (*center*) pals around with Sammy Davis Jr. and Frank Sinatra at Eli's The Place for Steak. *Marc Schulman.*

one Sunday, when Mayor Richard J. Daley arrived unannounced and asked for Eli. "After the mayor left without eating, my dad added Sunday to his workweek," said Eli's son Marc Schulman.

The steakhouse became more and more renowned and attracted the likes of Liza Minnelli, influential columnist Irv Kupcinet and a young prosecutor named James R. Thompson, who would go on to become Illinois's governor, later giving Schulman credit for encouraging his political career. Still, Schulman would close the restaurant every year on Mother's Day, Father's Day and for three weeks over the Christmas holidays to have time with his family.

But that's not the end of the story. In the late '70s, Schulman decided to make cheesecake the signature dessert at his steakhouse. After experimenting with several different recipes and testing them on patrons, he settled on a rich, cream cheese–based version with an all-butter cookie crust. The cheesecake made its big debut in 1980 at the first Taste of Chicago, which Schulman helped organize and promote. The dessert was so successful that

Eli Schulman, Rich Melman and Don Roth, three Chicago restaurant powerbrokers, discuss the first Taste of Chicago with Mayor Jane Byrne in 1980. *Marc Schulman.*

the company shifted focus, closed Eli's The Place for Steak in 2005 and launched a cheesecake business. Today, that huge enterprise is run out of Eli's Cheesecake World (6701 West Forest Preserve Drive), which includes a bakery, café and retail store (with guided tours). Eli's cheesecakes have become de rigueur at everything from family birthday parties to presidential inaugurations.

DON ROTH (1913–2003)

Don Roth, who ran the group of Blackhawk Restaurants, was a showman with extensive experience in advertising, marketing and entertainment booking before becoming a restaurateur. "It's a business, like any other," he said, "and it has to emphasize packaging, promotion and marketing to lure customers." When he took over the legendary Blackhawk from his father, Otto, in 1944, Don introduced dinner and dancing to big band and swing music that was broadcast live over the radio. The Blackhawk débuted with Carlton Coon, Joe Sanders and their Kansas City Nighthawks, which became the house band, and went on to feature many prominent entertainers, including Louis Prima, Glenn Miller, the Marx Brothers and Perry Como.

Live music catapulted the Blackhawk to national fame. After that ran its course, Roth shifted gears in 1952 by removing the band stage and declaring, "The food's the show." Part of the show was a roving cart with prime rib, cut tableside. More memorable is the spinning salad bowl, assembled and dressed tableside in an aluminum bowl set spinning in a bed of ice.

Roth continued to innovate, launching many campaigns and special events at the Blackhawk. He featured different European cuisines, month by month, and invited famous chefs from around the world to create food festivals. He converted the lower-level businessman's grill into the Indian Room, where Chief White Eagle told stories and taught children sign

Don Roth prepares a spinning salad at the Blackhawk, being careful "not to bruise the tender greens." Buster Keaton is seated on the right. *University of Illinois at Chicago Library.*

After removing its stage, the Blackhawk continued to innovate: art exhibits, fashion shows, kids' programs and more. For years, it catered American Airlines' inflight meals. *University of Illinois at Chicago Library.*

language. Later, he converted that room into the Old Frontier, where servers in cowboy attire served chuck wagon meals. He also instituted Jazz at Five; art exhibits; shuttle service to cultural and sporting events; a men's-only Executive Suite, with a copper fireplace and leather-paneled walls; men's and women's fashion shows; and a Wine Library.

Roth was also a shrewd businessman who kept an eye on costs. He stuck with a limited menu, which gave him greater control over production costs, and served simple food that was relatively easy to prepare. He was wont to employ young, enthusiastic and inexpensive college students. And he was always on the lookout for more opportunities, such as catering food for first-class American Airlines flights.

Roth was especially devoted to keeping the Loop lively and appealing to shoppers and diners. He supported Loop Alive, Mayor Jane Byrne's program to entice people downtown during the cold month of February by offering special events, extended business hours and restaurant discounts. And he was instrumental in launching Taste of Chicago in 1980.

ARNIE MORTON (1922–2005)

Arnie Morton is known as the man who created Morton's The Steakhouse chain, now with more than seventy restaurants around the world. The first one, at 1050 North State Street, still attracts large crowds of diners seeking that genuine Chicago steak experience.

From the age of fifteen, Morton worked in the restaurant business, starting as a busboy at his father's South Side restaurant called Morton's near Fifty-Fifth Street and Lake Park Avenue. Open from 1933 until 1971, this antecedent of Morton's The Steakhouse used the tagline "An Adventure in Good Eating." In the '50s, Morton followed his father's footsteps and opened his first restaurant, Walton Walk, on Walton Street near Michigan Avenue. In the '60s, Morton led the development of the Playboy Clubs and resorts. He then partnered with Klaus Fritsch and opened Arnie's at 1030 North State Street in the '70s. It was a sophisticated place and lasted until 1993 or 1994. Meanwhile, the partners opened Morton's The Steakhouse in the same building in 1978. The trademark of this new restaurant was giant potatoes and enormous steaks, a formula that reportedly did not take off until Frank Sinatra dined there and liked it so much that he became a regular when he was in town.

Morton went on to create many other restaurants, including Zorine's Club La Mer (named after his wife), a high-end French seafood restaurant, with famed chef Jean Banchet of Le Français. His wide knowledge of and connections in the restaurant business drove him to help develop Taste of Chicago, working with Eli Schulman, Mayor Jane Byrne and others. The first festival was held on July 4, 1980, on Michigan Avenue. About 100,000 people were expected to attend, but more than 250,000 showed up. Moved to Grant Park, the extremely popular festival continues to this day.

Arnie Morton got his start in the business by working at his father's restaurant in Hyde Park, promoted as "An Adventure in Good Eating." *Eric Bronsky.*

One reviewer called Morton "an-idea-a-minute" man, and another compared him to a Cuisinart that never stopped spinning. He was one of the first to push Navy Pier as a tourist attraction, and Mayor Richard M. Daley called him a "trailblazing entrepreneur."

GENE SAGE (1926–1999)

Gene Sage is remembered as a hardworking restaurateur with a talent for engaging promotions. He got into restauranting almost by accident. On a visit to Chicago, he decided to help his father, who had just opened a restaurant downtown. A few days led to a few months, which led to a year, which led to a career.

And what a career. Through the years, Sage opened nine Chicago-area restaurants, including Mon Petit; Sage's on State; Sage's East in the Lake Shore Drive Hotel; Eugene's; and Artists and Writers in the Playboy Building. Many of his restaurants were in the Gold Coast, which helped earn him the reputation as "pioneer of the singles bar." He opened his first restaurant in 1955, and his last one closed in 1997.

Sage was known for his hands-on management style, long hours and attention to detail, all of which led to tough standards and even some plates broken in anger. He worked against drunk driving and the overconsumption of alcohol at his restaurants. That included paying taxi fares for customers unfit to drive home and training sessions for servers on how to avoid overserving customers.

He also had a fun side and threw innumerable promotions, celebrity fundraisers and special events. At an indoor picnic, he had participants sitting on the floor as they ate boxed lunches. At A Night at the Races, he gave restaurant patrons play money to bet on several horse races at makeshift betting windows, with prizes awarded for the winners.

In the end, the things that counted the most are quality and integrity, Sage insisted. "We've seen nouvelle cuisine with raspberry sauce on everything come and go. We've seen showmanship come and go. We've seen a lot of things come and go, but what it comes down to is good food and careful service at an honest price," he told the *Tribune* in 1987.

PETER KOGEONES (1930–1990)

The gregarious Peter Kogeones, a Zorba the Greek–like character, was affectionately known as the "Mayor of Greektown" because he did so much to help establish the thriving restaurant district on South Halsted Street.

Kogeones came to Chicago from southern Greece in 1955 at the age of twenty-five and partnered with a family member at Diana Grocery, a small shop at 310 South Halsted Street. They added a few tables in the rear to make it a restaurant and later moved the establishment to 130 South Halsted Street.

In 1972, Kogeones opened his own full-fledged restaurant, Dianna's Opaa, at 212 South Halsted Street. The unusual spellings were meant to distinguish his place from others. The restaurant was a bit run-down, but Kogeones's shenanigans made up for that. He would welcome customers with a friendly pat on the back—or a kiss for the ladies. He would lead

Diana Grocery and Restaurant (130 South Halsted Street) was run by Peter Kogeones, who would dance, serve free drinks and kiss the ladies. *University of Illinois at Chicago Library.*

acrobatic Greek dances with a glass of water balanced on his head. And if there was a line in front of his restaurant, as was typical on weekends, he would ply patrons with wine or ouzo to encourage them to wait for a table.

Insisting on good personal service, Kogeones would discourage servers from standing around together. But he might have had an ulterior motive for doing this. He once told a restaurant reviewer, with a wink, "To prevent a coup, any assembly of more than three waiters is forbidden!" That same night, as he bantered his way around the restaurant, he told one table of regulars, "The food here is delicious…if you don't think so, get out!"

Guests who were on their way out were not allowed to leave until Kogeones shook their hands. "Thank you," he shouted. "Come again! God bless America!" Kogeones embodied the Greeks' sense of hospitality, veneration

FROM THE FILM *"Dream of Kings"*

Peter Kogeones, "Mayor of Greektown," was quite a showman. He appeared in the 1969 film *A Dream of Kings*, starring Anthony Quinn (*with hat*). *Author's collection.*

of visitors and generosity toward guests. And he played the minor role of Argelo in the 1969 dramatic movie *A Dream of Kings*, staring Anthony Quinn.

Kogeones died in 1990, and Dianna's Opaa closed in 1993. Both events were taken as evidence that Greektown was in decline, but the restaurants there remain vibrant to this day.

GORDON SINCLAIR (1935–)

What drove Gordon Sinclair into the restaurant business? "Well, I had been unemployed for over a year and needed to make a living," Sinclair replied. The former public relations executive had been fired from his previous job "for being too flamboyant," as Sinclair put it. "I guess my pocket-squares were too fancy."

After he spent some time being unemployed, someone at a dinner party said he was looking for a partner to open a restaurant, and Sinclair signed up. "Later the partner backed out," Sinclair recounted, "but by then I had already told everyone I was opening a restaurant, so I did, to save face."

The forty-year-old budding restaurateur scouted locations on his bike and settled on 512 North Clark Street in a run-down part of town. To learn the business while fixing up the "dump" he had leased, Sinclair went to work for famed restaurateur Gene Sage at Mon Petit. There, Sinclair learned that he "liked wearing a tuxedo and orchestrating evenings."

When Gordon finally opened in 1976, patrons who arrived by cab would ask the driver to wait until they verified that the place was legit. But the restaurant was wildly successful, demonstrating that when it comes to restaurants, it's not all about location, location, location.

Over the restaurant's twenty-three years, Sinclair hired fourteen head chefs, including some renowned ones such as Michael Kornick, Giuseppe Scurato and Michael Foley. The chef turnover brought additional publicity and kept the menu fresh. As the restaurant thrived, it raised the bar for other Chicago eateries.

Sinclair pioneered several restaurant practices. He offered half orders of entrées, which encouraged people to try more things. He claimed to be the first restaurant in Chicago to use a credit card to guarantee a reservation. He introduced shared seating, where diners who were not acquainted were

Gordon Sinclair turned the rundown St. Regis Hotel coffee shop into the chic Gordon. This was the restaurant's first location. Later, Gordon moved a couple of doors north. *Gordon Sinclair.*

offered seats at a common "Gordon's Table." (After meeting that way, one couple got married, Sinclair said.) And he asked diners not to speak on their cellphones while dining. This has been misreported as a cellphone ban, Sinclair complained. "We simply asked patrons to turn off their phones or leave them with the bartender, who would take any calls and alert the customer if it was important." (At this time, cellphones were the size of a brick, and had no answering-machine features.)

"Gordon was demanding but fun to work for, a bit eccentric but larger than life," said Rick Carbaugh, who worked with Sinclair from 1978 to 1982. "He flew by the seat of his pants but learned along the way."

In the '90s, Sinclair opened several other restaurants, including one in Jupiter, Florida, and another in Lake Forest, where he hired Charlie Trotter, something that turned out to be the young chef's first big break. Rather than selling his restaurant when he retired in 1999, Sinclair closed it. He knew that Gordon would never be the same without Gordon.

MICHAEL FOLEY (1955–)

In 1981, twenty-six-year old Michael Foley opened a contemporary American, dark wood and softly lit restaurant called Printers Row at 550 South Dearborn Street. It was a daring move since the run-down Printers Row neighborhood, full of abandoned warehouses and former publishing plants, had been declared by the city as "blighted." But the restaurant flourished on the strength of Foley's creative cooking and brightly flavored fare, such as vegetable paella or tuna seared with Chinese molasses. Or how about clam bisque flavored with saffron or tequila and lime–cured King salmon, served atop a mound of cold black beans, spiced with cumin and a cilantro pesto sauce?

Eating at Printers Row was adventuresome, and the menu was unpredictable. Venison and game were popular. "When the talented chef is featuring rabbit, I hop right in," wrote Murphy H. in an online review in 2000. Others flew over for the quail, squab and grouse. One reviewer said he would eat there just for the desserts.

A television crew showed up to tape Foley in 1984 for a show called *Great Chefs of Chicago*. At that time, reviewers on both coasts might have laughed at the idea that Chicago had great chefs, but Foley was evidence that Chicago was developing into a culinary capital. At the same time, Foley was very involved in the community, for instance hosting the Food Tent at the annual *Chicago Tribune* Printers Row Lit Fest, where chefs demonstrated their skills and passersby won prizes for guessing the chefs' favorite books.

Foley stressed local ingredients, and for a time, Printers Row raised eyebrows by carrying only American wine. Over the years, Foley opened additional restaurants, including Foley's (211 East Ohio Street) and Le Perroquet (where he attempted to revive the hallowed French landmark). He also opened a winery-brewery partnership and ran an organic farm.

After Printers Row closed in 2005, Foley went on to found Vegetable Alchemy, a firm that works at turning plant-based ingredients into delicious foods, thereby contributing to a healthier lifestyle. He continues to advocate for buying local and eating healthy through his writing, public presentations and consulting services.

CHARLIE TROTTER (1959–2013)

Charlie Trotter was obsessed with excellence, whether it came to sourcing ingredients, creating imaginative dishes or working outside the box. This culinary-school dropout credits unforgettable meals at The Bakery and Le Français for turning him on to a lifetime of cooking. He compared his cooking style to improvisational jazz, claiming never to repeat a dish. He and his restaurants, books and television shows won umpteen awards.

Incredibly, Trotter was self-taught through trial and error, cooking for friends, apprenticeships, several different jobs at dozens of restaurants and—most enjoyable of all—eating out a lot, all of this in the United States and France. He opened his eponymous restaurant in 1987, stressing French cooking techniques but incorporating an eclectic mix of international tastes, influences and ingredients. Some of his dishes defied categorization and would send diners scurrying for a dictionary, though they had grown to trust Trotter's touch. Chicagoans had never seen the likes of pickled kohlrabi and crispy lotus root; braised veal cheek with porcini mushrooms, veal tongue, sweetbreads and confit of turnip; poached breast of squab with black cardamom–infused carrots; and grilled Nantucket Bay scallops with candied kumquats.

Charlie Trotter's, the restaurant, was located at 816 West Armitage Avenue in a beautifully restored 1880s mansion, with limited seating. It was the talk of the town for more than a decade—and a table there was

Charlie Trotter credited meals at The Bakery, cooked by the legendary chef Louis Szathmary (*with hat*), with getting him interested in the culinary arts. *Author's collection.*

among the hardest reservations to snag. Dinners consisted of dégustations of six or more courses. The food is remembered as French cooking with American ingredients, often influenced by what was available at the produce market. Trotter was "gifted in creating dishes in a new realm with sometimes disparate ingredients and eclectic foreign influences," wrote Camille Staff in *The Eclectic Gourmet Guide to Chicago.*

Besides being remembered for his creative cooking and delectable dishes, Trotter will be credited for giving a great deal to his profession and to the city of Chicago. He showed how a chef could win in the restaurant business. He built his name into a brand, like a top designer logo. He set up a foundation that awarded culinary scholarships. And he frequently invited underprivileged children, not only to eat at his restaurants but also to learn about the art of cooking, the work of a chef and the restaurant business. "For years, Trotter introduced public school students to what a fine meal is, and how to recognize and appreciate good cooking," said Monique Tranchevent, director of L'École Franco-Americaine de Chicago, which operated out of Abraham Lincoln Public Elementary School. "He'd take the students into the kitchen, explain everything about the sauces....And then the students would sit down

Charlie Trotter's, in a beautifully restored Victorian mansion at 816 West Armitage Avenue, was considered one of the country's best restaurants. *Eric Bronsky.*

and enjoy the full meal. Trotter was professional and, at the same time, friendly. I'm sure the students will always remember their experience with him."

In the end, Trotter, a tough taskmaster, decided not to pass the torch or sell his restaurant. Instead, much to the chagrin of his fervent followers, he closed his restaurant in 2012 on its twenty-fifth anniversary. He died unexpectedly one year later. The *New York Times* said in its obituary that Trotter had made Chicago "a must restaurant destination."

DOUG SOHN (1962–)

Doug Sohn is Chicago's all-time top dog of hot dogs, or "encased meats," which he refers to as "the two finest words in the English language." Although he studied culinary arts at Kendall College, Sohn wasn't planning to open a restaurant. "That was never a goal of mine; it just kinda happened," he said.

The idea grew out of frequent hot dog lunches around Chicago that made Sohn realize most places, for one reason or another, got it wrong. "I wanted to restore the reputation of the Chicago hot dog and to have a place where you could get all kinds of different sausages."

Sohn quit his day job in 2001 and launched Schleppy's: The Bulvan. Well, that was going to be the name of his place, until he wisely decided to follow his dad's suggestion of "Hot Doug's." It was different than any other hot dog restaurant: full focus on sausage (not hamburgers, chicken, burritos…); a wide variety of encased meats, including many gourmet options; fun music; and friendly customer service.

"You can't beat places on price, convenience or speed," he said. "But you can treat people better."

To ensure that, Sohn stood at the front counter virtually the entire time the restaurant was open and greeted every customer as he took their order. This allowed for some pleasant banter, as well as the development of some true friendships. The restaurant resulted in more than a few romances and even some marriage proposals. Sohn even officiated at one of the weddings that blossomed out of his restaurant.

Many customers returned repeatedly, and others joined what grew into a huge fan club. About one hundred fans felt so enamored of the restaurant that they got a tattoo of Hot Doug's logo. Sohn rewarded these diehards with free hot dogs for life.

When asked whether he got a Hot Doug's tattoo, Sohn replied, "Why would I do that? I already get free food there." It was this wry sense of humor that really drove the place. When Sohn's brother asked him whether he should sell hamburgers, Sohn replied, "I'll know in six months." Of Barbara Louise Tyksinski, his longtime partner, he quipped, "If you don't think that the main reason I asked her out is that her initials are 'BLT,' then you don't know me that well." (Riffing off that, Sohn dedicated his book *Hot Doug's, The Book*, written with Kate DeVivo, to "BLT.")

Kidding aside, Sohn was determined to run his sausage emporium on his own terms. He kept limited hours—about six hours a day, six days a week. He accepted only cash to avoid the extra work and "profit-sharing" that credit cards require. He treated his workers well, so they would stay, some of them for most of the thirteen years the restaurant was open. He never watered down the Hot Doug's experience by franchising or selling out. And he got out on top.

Since closing the restaurant in 2014, Sohn has been watching an inordinate amount of baseball, consulting about restaurant management and customer service, and working on a couple of books. He still selects and orders meats for Hot Doug's, which lives on as a concession stand at Wrigley Field. "I wanted to unplug," he said, "but they had me with 'free pass to the ballpark.'"

———⬤⬤⬤———

Of course, there are many other restaurant movers and shakers who provided Chicago residents and visitors rich, memorable culinary experiences. Thanks for the memories and the meals.

I think it's safe to say that I speak for all the restaurateurs and entrepreneurs, chefs and servers, owners and patrons of bygone restaurants when I encourage you to eat out da Chicago way: "Early and often!"

Bibliography

Books

Bizzarri, Amy. *Iconic Chicago Dishes, Drinks and Desserts.* Charleston, SC: The History Press, 2016.

Block, Daniel, and Howard Rosing. *Chicago: A Food Biography.* Lanham, MD: Powman & Littlefield, 2015.

Bronsky, Eric, and Neal Samors. *Chicago's Classic Restaurants: Past, Present and Future.* Chicago: Chicago Books Press, 2011.

Bundy, Beverly. *The Century in Food: America's Fads and Favorites.* Portland, OR: Collectors Press, 2002.

Candeloro, Dominic. *Italians in Chicago.* Charleston, SC: Arcadia Publishing, 1999.

Cotter, Bill. *Chicago's 1933–34 World's Fair: A Century of Progress.* Charleston, SC: Arcadia Publishing, 2015.

Cutler, Irving. *The Jews of Chicago: From Shtetl to Suburb.* Urbana: University of Illinois Press, 1996.

Davros, Michael George. *Greeks in Chicago.* Charleston, SC: Arcadia Publishing, 2009.

Drury, John. *Dining in Chicago.* New York: John Day Co., 1931.

Duis, Perry. *Challenging Chicago: Coping with Everyday Life, 1837–1920.* Urbana: University of Illinois Press, 1998.

Gale, Edwin Oscar, *Reminiscences of Early Chicago and Vicinity.* Chicago: Fleming H. Revell Co., 1902.

Ganakos, Alexa. *Greektown Chicago: Its History, Its Recipes.* St. Louis, MO: Bradley Publishing Co., 2005.

Grossman, James, Ann Durkin Keating and Janice Reiff, eds. *Encyclopedia of Chicago.* Chicago: University of Chicago Press, 2004.

Haddix, Carol Mighton, ed. *Chicago Cooks.* Chicago: Les Dames d'Escoffier Chicago, 2007.

Haddix, Carol Mighton, Bruce Kraig and Colleen Taylor Sen, eds. *The Chicago Food Encyclopedia.* Urbana: University of Illinois Press, 2017.

Heinen, Joseph C., and Susan Barton. *Lost German Chicago.* Charleston, SC: Arcadia Publishing, 2009.

Hoekstra, Dave. *The People's Palace: Soul Food Restaurants and Reminiscences from the Civil Rights Era to Today.* Chicago: Chicago Review Press, 2015.

Iversen, Jean. *Local Flavors: Restaurants that Shaped Chicago's Neighborhoods.* Evanston, IL: Northwestern University Press, 2018.

Lynch, Christopher. *Chicago's Midway Airport, The First Seventy-Five Years.* Chicago: Lake Claremont Press, 2002.

Mariani, John. *America Eats Out.* New York: William Morrow and Co., 1991.

Nager, Victoria, and Valerie Nager. *Dining Lite Chicago.* Chicago: Brooke-Brandon Communications, 1989.

Pacyga, Dominic. *Chicago: A Biography.* Chicago: University of Chicago Press, 2009.

Pierce, Bessie Louise. *As Others See Chicago: Impressions of Visitors, 1673–1933.* Chicago: University of Chicago Press, 1933.

Pillsbury, Richard. *From Boarding House to Bistro: The American Restaurant Then and Now.* Boston: Unwin Hyman, 1990.

Pocius, Marilyn. *A Cook's Guide to Chicago.* Chicago: Lake Claremont Press, 2006.

Schulman, Maureen, et al. *The Eli's Cheesecake Cookbook.* Chicago: Eli's Cheesecake Co., 2015.

Sheahan, James, and Louis Kurz. *Chicago Illustrated.* Chicago: Jevne & Almini, 1866.

Sohn, Doug, with Kate DeVivo. *Hot Doug's: The Book.* Chicago: Midway, 2013.

Soucek, Gayle. *Marshall Field's: The Store that Helped Build Chicago.* Charleston, SC: The History Press, 2010.

Stagg, Camille. *The Eclectic Gourmet Guide to Chicago.* Birmingham, AL: Menasha Ridge Press, 2000.

Ward, James. *Restaurants: Chicago Style.* Boston: CBI Publishing Co., 1979.

Zurawski, Joseph. *Polish Chicago: Our History, Our Recipes.* St. Louis, MO: Bradley Publishing Co., 2007.

Websites

checkplease.wttw.com
chefdb.com
chicagocollections.org
chicago.curbed.com
chicago.eater.com
chicagoist.com
chicagology.com
chicagosextinctbusinesses.com
chicagotonight.wttw.com/recurring-segments/ask-geoffrey
craigslostchicago.com
forgottenchicago.com
frenchvirtualcafe.blogspot.com
gayot.com/closed-restaurants/chicago-area
restaurant-ingthroughhistory.com
therestaurantproject.wordpress.com

Periodicals

Chicago Daily News
Chicago Defender
Chicago Magazine
Chicago Reader
Chicago Sun-Times
Chicago Tribune
Crain's Chicago Business
Daily Herald
Daily Southtown
DNA Info
Economist
Gazette Chicago
Hyde Park Herald
New York Times
Time magazine
Time Out Chicago

Restaurant Guides

(print and online; multiple years)
Gayot, Michelin, Open Table, TripAdvisor, Yelp, Zagat, Zomato.

Index

Greg Borzo is an award-winning journalist, public-relations professional and author.

He has worked full time as a writer at *Modern Railroads*, *Traffic World*, Business Word, Field Museum, *American Medical News* and, most recently, the University of Chicago's News Office. He has written several books, including *The Chicago "L"*; *Chicago Cable Cars*; *RAGBRAI: America's Favorite Bicycle Ride; Where to Bike Chicago*; and *Chicago's Fabulous Fountains*.

Borzo earned a BA in cultural anthropology from Grinnell College and an MA in journalism from Northwestern University's Medill School of Journalism. He's a reviewer for the Chicago Writer's Association, an instructor at Oakton Community College and the program chair of the Society of Midland Authors.

Borzo loves to share his knowledge of and enthusiasm for Chicago. To that end, he's a member of the Chicago Tour-Guide Professional Association and has led walking, bike and bus tours for the Chicago History Museum, Chicago Cycling Club, Forgotten Chicago, Women Bike Chicago and many other organizations. Also, he's given hundreds of PowerPoint presentations about Chicago at libraries, schools, civic organizations, senior centers, clubs, museums and other groups.

ABOUT THE AUTHOR

Borzo lives in the South Loop to better enjoy Chicago's culture and history; art and architecture; music and museums; and everything else the city has to offer—in particular, restaurants! He would welcome speaking engagements, tour requests and restaurant invitations—as well as any reactions to this book. (E-mail him at gborzo@comcast.net.)